Permaculture

An Essential Guide to Incorporating Backyard Homesteading, Greenhouses, Urban Gardening, Solar Power Systems, Composting, and More for Sustainable Living

Contents

Introduction

At its most basic level, permaculture is an environmentally friendly approach to farming and gardening that you can use as much or as little as you want, integrating it into your lifestyle. Permaculture teaches you how to incorporate an awareness of the environment into every aspect of your life to mitigate the negative impact on the environment. The central idea of permaculture is this: you need to learn how to work *with* nature instead of against it. You want your daily activities to nurture the earth, its creatures, and its flora in all their miraculous variety. This book provides a thorough, detailed discussion of permaculture and its many facets.

This book is a goldmine for beginning permaculture enthusiasts. Within these pages, you will learn about reducing your environmental footprint, recycling household waste, and reusing common everyday items. You'll also learn about different types of gardens—both urban and rural—as well as greenhouses, solar power systems, and composting. You'll learn how to make your permaculture endeavor self-contained and self-sustaining, balancing inflows with outflows. Finally, you'll learn the many intricate details of water management, space management, and utilizing animals on your permaculture property. This book is crammed full of information for anyone wanting to get started with permaculture. If this is a topic you are interested in, then this book is a perfect starting point.

The book provides a comprehensive discussion with all of the latest information, broken down into easily manageable chapters. You will find all that you need to transform any outdoor space, large or small, or even make the most of an apartment, even if you do not have a yard. It will also stimulate the imagination of more experienced permaculture enthusiasts, offering tips and pointers on improving projects that have already been started. You'll learn new techniques and strategies, and, at the same time, you'll absorb the tenets of the core ethical foundations of the discipline and its most powerful principles. Finally, you'll learn how to apply these principles and tenets and how to tease out new implications in a variety of ways.

You'll walk away from this book informed, energized, and enthusiastic about making a difference in the fight against climate change and the task of raising environmental awareness across the globe. This book will change the way that you look at nature and ecosystems.

Chapter 1: Defining Permaculture

Permaculture. It's an interesting word and one that many people recognize. But what does it actually mean? To be honest, there is no single clear-cut definition of the word. Through the years, many definitions have been put forward. The term was first coined in the 1970s by Bill Mollison and David Holmgren. It was originally intended as a verbal contraction of the words "permanent" and "agriculture." The concept was later expanded to include "culture" instead of "agriculture."

The intent was to convey a notion of permanency or sustainability, first in humanity's agricultural endeavors and later in its cultural ones. One of the first formal attempts at definition came from Bill Mollison himself: "The conscious design and maintenance of agriculturally productive systems which have the diversity, stability, and resilience of natural ecosystems. It is the harmonious integration of the landscape with people, providing their food, energy, shelter, and other material and non-material needs in a sustainable way" (*hat tip to Modern Farmer for the quote*).

In other words, permaculture starts as an agricultural attempt to live in harmony with nature. It also uses nature and its systems as models for other human endeavors. At this point, it expands to pervade our concept of culture. To model a business after an organism or an economy after an ecosystem, you are thinking like a permaculture enthusiast (also called a "permie").

Today, permaculture is far more than just a novel approach to agriculture. It is, instead, a philosophical approach to living that can influence many different aspects of your life.

The History of Permaculture

Bill Mollison and David Holmgren are widely recognized as the founders of the permaculture movement, but it does have roots that go back further. For example, in 1964, P.A. Yeomans of Australia authored the book "Water for Every Farm," which proved influential for the permaculture movement. Another influential contributor was Joseph Russell Smith, a man who ran several experiments on effectively raising crops using mixed systems of animals, trees, and other plants.

However, Mollison and Holmgren were the ones who really put the philosophy of permaculture on the map with their 1978 book, *Permaculture One*. Bill Mollison, a professor, studied and taught in the fields of environmental psychology and biogeography at the University of Tasmania. While there, he met a graduate student named David Holmgren. Working together, they developed many of the principles and methods of permaculture that are still used worldwide today. Although many scientific circles have criticized Mollison's and Holmgren's work and permaculture practices in general, the permaculture field remains a popular approach to holistic living and agriculture.

The Three Basic Tenets of Permaculture

Permaculture provides a philosophical approach to agriculture and living. It is grounded in three basic tenets.

1. Care for the Earth: This is pretty basic and self-explanatory. We have but one planet to call home, and we can't afford to ruin it. That would be disastrous for humanity and all other living things on the planet. Permaculture calls on us to care for the Earth so that we can continue to live on it in harmony.

2. Care for the People: "No man is an island, entire of itself." (*J. Donne*) We live in our respective communities, large and small. The permaculture approach encourages us to engage with our society to better our community, including the global community of which we are all a part.

3. Take Your Fair Share and Return the Excess: This last tenet encourages us to take what we need and not just whatever we want, returning what we do not need so that others can benefit too. That includes people, animals, and plant life. If we have excess, we are encouraged to return it to the system so that the system can grow, and everyone can share in it.

Other Permaculture Considerations

The distinct elements of permaculture differ from the three tenets. They constitute the practical consequences of applying the three tenets. However, there is no uniform consent on which elements are the most relevant and foundational. One permaculture enthusiast might endorse all while another may only work with some or one or two. That does not mean that one is right, and another is wrong. Using the elements means doing what is best for you and your environment to live within the three tenets and promote the permaculture movement.

5 Elements of Permaculture Philosophy

As an example, consider the following set of five elements of permaculture (courtesy of *Modern Farmer*).

Closed-Loop Systems: A closed-loop system is a system that uses every available resource and avoids all waste. It is a "Closed Loop" because that which is within the system loops around through the system and never exits. Look at a farm and divide it into inputs and outputs. Labor and fertilizer, as well as seed from your hand, would constitute inputs. The food you eat from the farm would constitute outputs. Think about growing plants from seeds and then using the seeds from these plants for your crops the next year. Or feeding crops to animals and using the manure to fertilize the next growth. Closed-loop systems turn waste to their advantage, and everything in them has a purpose.

Perennial Crops: Using perennial plants instead of annuals spares the soil from repeated tilling. Soil needs time to build up nutrients, and constant farming can strip the soil of fertility.

Multiple Functions: This element advocates getting as many uses as possible out of each and every component of your permaculture system. For example, your fruit-bearing trees can provide shade for plants that need it while serving as a windbreak for another part of the yard.

Eco-Earthworks: The flow and use of water are a major concern. Often, to redirect flowing rainwater or runoff, earthworks can be built into the ground. Terraces can be dug out on steep land, while more moderate slopes can be served with shallow ditches called swales. It all serves one purpose: using the naturally provided water to the best effect, collecting and utilizing rainwater and other natural water sources while eliminating water waste.

Let Nature Do the Work for You: It's a common maxim, "work smarter, not harder." Permaculture takes this and gives it a new twist. You don't have to work so much if you can get nature to do the work for you. For example, one can use livestock like chickens and set them loose to clear an area of unwanted pests while they are also cutting the grass. Once the chickens are well-fed, they can be moved to another area. The area that is left will be removed of plants, pests, and weeds and fertilized by chicken poop. Now, you can go ahead and plant without having to do all of the proviso work by yourself.

Why Is Permaculture Important?

Now that you have some idea of what permaculture entails, maybe we should talk about why you should consider adopting it as a lifestyle. Why is it important for you? What are its most immediate benefits?

There are numerous advantages to adopting a permaculture lifestyle. First, it provides an excellent creative outlet. Gardening alone is a great form of physical activity. Applying permaculture principles to both gardening and your lifestyle makes both endeavors all the more rewarding.

Permaculture also helps your land become much more productive. This can help defray your costs of living and provide a sense of accomplishment. It can also help you reclaim damaged areas of your land and improve its aesthetic appeal. Not only do permaculture gardens provide an abundance of resources, but they also provide beauty.

Also, as you work on your property, you will acquire skills that will help you design and nurture any type of land to maximize its potential. It will become an acquired life skill. You will gain skills in both gardening methods and animal husbandry.

If you are already engaged in farming or gardening, adopting a permaculture approach can help reduce the work you have to do. This factor becomes all the more pronounced, the more you expand into other areas of your life.

As you learn to work with nature instead of against it, you can harness its natural force to ever greater effect. Capturing rainwater for gardening purposes is just one example of defraying utility costs.

Finally, you will become a more positive force for the benefit of the environment. You will reduce your personal environmental impact because what you produce yourself need not be produced elsewhere and then transported to you. This results in fewer fuel costs, less energy expended, and an all-around more sustainable environment. You will find yourself more in tune with your surrounding ecological systems, and instead of exploiting these systems, you will be able to live within them.

Difference between Organic Farming and Permaculture Lifestyle

Many people involved in permaculture split hairs, and rightly so, differentiating between the permaculture lifestyle and simple organic farming. How do they differ? How are they the same?

Both systems are rooted in environmental awareness. However, the depth of environmental impact in the mindset and lifestyles of the respective methods is what sets the two apart. Although permaculture is most assuredly influenced by organic farming, it takes several more steps down the path of environmental consideration.

Organic Farming

In organic farming, an emphasis is placed on using natural fertilizers and avoiding synthetic pesticides and other harmful chemicals. However, every crop grown and harvested will result in a loss of minerals and nutrients from the soil. As stated previously, you should try to keep your inputs lower than or equal to your outputs to build a rich and self-sustaining garden system.

Example of organic garden rows

Permaculture

Permaculture is different than organic gardening. It doesn't just use natural fertilizer; it uses on-site waste products as fertilizer. This lowers dependence on external inputs.

Permaculture also stresses planning and foresight in the design of your garden, especially concerning the required physical labor. This reduces energy input and difficult, repetitive work. Reducing ecological damage and developing an interesting, varied lifestyle of self-sufficiency can become a motivating closed loop. Permaculture seeks to harness the abilities of all types of people; it is not a system that relies solely on those who are young enough and strong enough for hard physical labor like digging.

Permaculture seeks to imitate nature. Plants are rarely planted in rows. Instead, they are grown together and become a complicated ecosystem interwoven in such a way as to conserve space, soil, and water. In a permaculture garden, natural energies such as sunshine, water, wind, and foliage are used and maximized.

Example of permaculture garden

A permaculture system does not seek to serve the nutritional needs of humans and humans alone. A functioning component of the larger environment is providing habitat and food for local birds and animals. Think about it. Which is more efficient? Spending all your time trying to keep "pesky" birds out of your garden and away from your seeds and tomatoes, or growing your garden with those animals in mind and accepting that some of your product will go to feed them? One path results in hours of potentially fruitless labor. The other involves a little bit of extra planning and planting, but fewer worries down the road, and your pest control can be naturally taken care of. The key is not deterring other wildlife but investigating what benefits additional wildlife can bring.

Another critical distinction between organic farming and permaculture is that permaculture goes beyond the simple act of growing food. It involves a philosophical approach to living that, if you allow it, can influence many aspects of your daily life.

As a dedicated permaculture enthusiast, you may find an opportunity to use the philosophical principles of permaculture in many unexpected ways. Being environmentally conscious when shopping is only the beginning. Perhaps you start by being a little more discerning about the products you purchase and how they affect the environment. Next, you develop the habit of recycling and reusing those products you once threw out without much thought: paper products get composted, egg cartons become seedling trays, and extra garbage containers can become rain receptacles for your garden. If you own a wood stove or fire pit, the ash from either of those can be a rich resource of phosphorous, beneficial to soil nutrition, for your garden. The principles of the permaculture philosophy can influence even your place of work. The only limit is the fertility of your imagination.

There is also a little more flexibility in a permaculture approach than in an organic one. Sometimes, a permaculture system uses products that are not as organic as they could be in the "purest" sense of the word. For example, you may have to go with a local resource that doesn't quite meet all the guidelines of "organic." You might use local waste products (like manure) because they are cheaper and more readily accessible than the products of certified organic sources. Alternatively, you might introduce interesting plants from a non-organic source and still be embracing the permaculture doctrine because you are increasing diversity. It's a question of weighing costs and rewards, balances and measures. It's a question of strategic, long-term thinking to build an environmentally sound way of life.

Chapter 2: The Ethics and Principles of Permaculture

Due to environmental abuse and mismanagement on a global scale, the human race now faces one of its greatest challenges. If we fail to meet this challenge, our very existence may be threatened. There is, however, hope. As a philosophy and way of life, permaculture offers us the chance to help shape our society into a more sustainable, eco-friendly culture.

The Three Tenets

There are three ethical principles or tenets that form the foundation of the philosophy and way of life embodied by permaculture:

Care for the Earth

We have only one planet. We cannot afford to abuse or misuse it. Many people take it for granted, but it is the source of all the resources we consume. If the planet dies, we die. It is that simple. It should be clear that as a custodian of the planet, you must care for and be considerate of all flora and fauna, all the waterways, and all the natural life on the planet, and that starts in your own backyard. You should always seek to increase biodiversity and regenerate fertility rather than maintain the status quo. With permaculture, you should constantly ask yourself whether your actions hurt or help the local environment. Is there a better, more ecologically sound, and more efficient method available? Can nature itself readily teach you how to solve your problem? By doing your part on a small scale, you are helping the planet as a whole.

Care for People

We live on a planet with an ever-increasing number of people. Of these, uncounted millions suffer from hunger and starvation. If you embrace the permaculture philosophy, you will begin to take responsibility for your own existence as a member of the human race. You will produce more and consume less. You can move away from consumerism and the notion that the acquisition and consumption of goods are the main goals in life. When you do this, you will naturally start to avoid those companies that prosper by exploiting people and nature. By making the best use of the products you have at your disposal, you will find there is much you can do to take care of yourself and others. When you grow your own food and reduce your purchases, you are not feeding into a system of exploitation. Not only does that mean that the rich are not getting richer, and the poor are not getting poorer; it also means you are not taking food from needy people in other countries.

Fair Share

When you properly care for the earth, it rewards you in kind. Nature gives you more plants and animals, healthier water and air, more biodiversity, and so much more. You benefit from all of that. Using the permaculture philosophy, you take what you need and not what you want. This not only reduces waste, but it also leaves more for other people. When more people engage in permaculture, there is less chance for exploitation in the production of food. When companies cannot wield power over you by offering cheap produce, the exploitation across the world is lessened, and there is more for everyone.

Nature responds by producing ever more resources which, when you have met your needs, you can reinvest back into your community. You can share food and skills, or maybe even financial assistance. This is what is meant by "fair share." You obtain what you need and give back the excess; you can return it to nature in the form of compost or to the community in the form of seeds and food.

The 12 Principles

One of the founders of permaculture, David Holmgren, put forward twelve design principles to give us some conceptual tools to build a better, more sustainable world and incorporate the permaculture philosophy into our lives.

1. **Observe and Interact:** If you become a conscientious observer of nature, not only will you reap the awards that come with observing its awesome natural beauty, but you will better learn how to move to a more environmentally conscious lifestyle. You will learn how to live greener and more ethically. You can study the movements of the wind, water, and sun, learning how they move across or through your land, and note the pattern of each. How should such information affect your design decisions?

Is there a portion of your yard that is shaded more than all the others? What plants will grow there more readily? Is there certain wildlife that ventures onto your land more frequently? What is their routine and life cycle? Is there anything that would have gone unnoticed had you built a garden without observing first?

2. Catch and Store Energy: A critical component of permaculture is the catching and storing of energy. The ultimate source of energy is the sun. If you learn how to catch and store that energy, whether it be in the growth of plant life or in other ways, you can reap incredible benefits on your path to a sustainable lifestyle. The most obvious store of energy is the aforementioned plant life. Such storage can serve many different functions; it can allow you to grow your own food, which will provide nutrition and energy. Also, dead plant matter can be composted to provide nutrition and energy to other plants. If you are raising livestock, it can provide food to them through grazing or winter stockpiling. Plants, especially trees, can provide firewood for heating and cooking. All of this is linked back to the sun, the ultimate source of energy, but the energy comes through the plant life on your homestead. The same is true of water. Rainwater is an amazing water source that can be collected and stored. Can you take advantage of natural streams, lakes, and other water sources? Can you use all of this water without wasting any? If you can capture and store sunlight and water, you are well on your way to a permaculture lifestyle.

3. Obtain a Yield: When you work, you want some form of reward or to feel like you've accomplished something. This is as true in permaculture as it is in any other endeavor. Such rewards can take the form of food for ourselves and our families or even our community. Or it can be something a little less tangible: the emotional satisfaction you get from a job well done, or even just the health benefits obtained from healthy eating. You might enjoy the beauty that nature brings; the towering green trees, the colorful flowers, or the animals and birds that are attracted to your garden. It is a good idea to make a list of what you want from your permaculture garden and keep the list handy, in order to direct your efforts towards those yields.

4. Apply Self-Regulation and Feedback: The next principle is all about bringing a certain level of discipline to your lifestyle and unleashing your inner scientist. Make an effort to evaluate and analyze everything you use in your home and garden. Study everything you bring in and ask questions about it. Can it be reused or recycled? Do you truly need it, or is it something you can do without? Basically, you want to use your "scientific mind" to cut back on your ecological footprint by regulating your consumption. As time passes, you can continue to analyze what feedback you get to improve your results. The goal is to discourage those kinds of activities harmful to the environment and, by studying the feedback, encourage beneficial activities. This need not only apply to physical waste; it can be applied to waste of time too. For example, do you find yourself making multiple trips out to your yard, some to feed animals, others to weed, and a final one to plant? Can you combine these trips and cut down on your waste? Track everything that you do and see where waste can be eliminated.

5. Use and Value Renewables: Permaculture emphasizes renewable resources over perishable ones. This most obviously applies to energy sources. A permaculture enthusiast will use solar panels or windmills, for instance, or choose a green supplier of energy. Although energy is a serious consideration, there is more to it than just installing a couple of solar panels. Permaculturalists seek out things like ecological building, soil conservation, planting perennial plants for food, incorporating seed saving with annuals, and coppicing, which is a technique of harvesting the regrowth of trees. The idea is to make the most effective use of nature's abundant resources and perpetuate their production.

6. Produce No Waste: The permaculture philosophy is very waste-conscious. The ideal you want to strive towards is no waste at all. Yes, if possible, you want to return all waste to the system to be recycled and reused by nature again. This requires considerable effort on your part. You'll have to look at the garbage you routinely dispose of and make some important decisions. You can reduce how much you buy, make wiser purchases, and develop a habit of reusing what you can and recycling the rest. Composting is one of the more valuable tools in your arsenal. You can compost food scraps, garden waste, and most organic waste products. You can also seek out companies that make an effort to know their products' whole life-cycle in terms of waste and reuse instead of those companies that make single-use products.

7. Design from Patterns to Details: This principle emphasizes the importance of top-down design. Look at the big picture first before focusing on the details. You must first think holistically, not only regarding your garden but also regarding your whole homestead and all areas of your life. Begin with principle one: Observe and Interact. Note the passing of the seasons and how that affects the local climate. Keep tabs on the weather and the soil patterns, the slope of the land, and your own activities. When you step back and observe such things, you can get a large-scale picture of what you can accomplish on your property and how to go about doing so. This also applies to your life in other areas of society. First, observe large-scale patterns and then fill in the details. You'll find it will improve your life considerably.

8. Integrate Don't Segregate: Plants thrive best in diverse collections that work together; these conditions are called polycultures. A similar idea is often applied to people under the banner of multiculturism and diversity. Both these examples represent this principle in action. Look at companion gardening, where different types of plants are grown together to attract bees or other beneficial insects, or to deter pests. Don't work against nature and separate your plants into neat columns and rows. That is unnecessary, and ultimately counterproductive. Mix your plants together—not haphazardly but keeping careful note of their respective functions in nature, and your ecosystem will reap the rewards.

9. Use Small, Slow Solutions: Start small and grow big. If you try to do too much at once, you'll likely become overwhelmed and may even give up before you have started. Start with just a few plants in a small area close to your house. Work on that, building it slowly using permaculture strategies and principles. Study it like a scientist and analyze your results. Did the strategies work as expected? Did you have to make any adjustments? What didn't work? Can you expand what did work and apply it to future projects? Keep going. Keep experimenting. And don't be afraid to fail. It is better to fail on a single small project and learn from that mistake than to suffer a disaster because of a critical mistake on a larger scale.

10. Use and Value Diversity: This principle is similar to the principle of "Integrate, Don't Segregate". The idea is to place great value on diversity. Ecosystems function more effectively and efficiently when more plants and animals of different kinds are represented. Different plants will perform different functions in the garden. Each one will build relationships with the others, making the group stronger, healthier, and more productive than any plant or group of plants would be alone. Look at what each plant or tree can bring to an ecosystem and think about how you could apply that to your garden. What do you need more of? What is hampering your ecosystem? What natural solution is there? A classic, often cited example of this is planting mashua under locust trees; the locust tree enriches the soil with nitrogen and provides a support structure for the mashua, and both plants benefit.

11. Use Edges and Value the Marginal: An edge is an area where two or more elements meet and mingle. For example, an edge might be where a forest canopy stops, and a meadow begins. There you will likely find a good number of flowers flourishing as they take advantage of the sunshine, air, and shade. Or perhaps it is where a riverbank ends, and a windblown plain begins. It may be the area where your homemade pond ends, and a group of your thirstier crops begin in your permaculture garden. These are the areas you do not necessarily plan for, but they will bring new ways of looking at your garden. As they grow and develop over time, go back to the first principle and observe what this marginal area brings to your garden and how you can integrate it.

12. Creatively Use and Respond to Change: Change is a part of life, but it is how you react to change that is in the interest of the permaculture philosophy. Permaculture is as much about planning for the future as it is in dealing with the now. We understand that through the years, our homesteads will change. You don't want to build a greenhouse that might be threatened by a falling tree or a rushing stream that will erode away its support. The permaculture philosophy urges you to consider all these factors. To remain viable, to remain stable, you must do these three things: embrace the change, understand the change, and prepare for the change. In short, you must work with change diligently and creatively. When designing your permaculture space, look to the future and imagine how the land will change over time. And, as the land does change over time, do not be afraid to change your plans with it.

Together with the three tenets, these twelve principles provide the driving force and the conceptual toolset that propels the permaculture movement forward. Understanding these ideas and putting them into practice will help you develop your own permaculture homestead, one that is both beautiful and useful, that helps preserve both the planet and your community, and that will reward you for the rest of your life.

Chapter 3: The Benefits of Permaculture

Permaculture isn't a new development, although the term was only coined in the 1970s. It returns to the mindset of early societies where the goal was to make the earth your ally, not your enemy, in agriculture. In the process, you learned to minimize the resources you used, maximize each one's variable functions, and use organic material as fertilizer. As a result of handing down the wisdom of those early societies, permaculture gardens and farms today are rich in produce and other products that serve many purposes.

15 Benefits of Permaculture

Permaculture has a great number of benefits. What follows is not a comprehensive list, but it does give you an idea of what permaculture can do.

Permaculture Produces Healthier Food

Supermarket produce is not nearly as nutritious as food straight from your garden. This is because produce starts losing nutrients shortly after it's harvested. Think of all that time it takes to get the food from the farm to the grocery store. Three days? A week? Sometimes, it is even longer than that. All of that leads to deterioration of the nutrient density of the produce. If you grow your food at home, you won't suffer that loss.

Many modern farms are nonorganic. That is, they use artificial pesticides and fertilizers to help the plants grow. These chemicals can harm the soil, decreasing its nutrient density, leading to lower nutrient density in crops grown upon it. This has led to a growing concern regarding the nutritional value found in the current food supply.

Artificial chemicals in fertilizers often find their way into our natural water supplies. When concentrated, it can lead to the poisoning of even the largest bodies of water, killing aquatic life or entering our food supply.

Permaculture Reduces Costs

There are many different ways that permaculture will help you save money. These include:

• **Reducing Fertilizer Costs**: Permaculture uses only the natural products and processes of an ecosystem to fertilize it. For example, it is common practice to compost garden waste and recycle that as fertilizer for your garden. Each time you do that, you save yourself the expense of purchasing store-bought fertilizer. Those savings add up over time.

• **Reducing Food Costs**: The more food you grow, the less you need to purchase at the store. Again, this saves you money that adds up over time.

• **Reducing Utility Costs**: When it gets hot in the summer, you can spend a lot on air conditioning. The same goes for heating costs in the colder months. A permaculture garden can create natural shade for a garden or home. Trees and bushes can act as windbreakers. Employing structures such as earth homes or earthships, you can live in a home that is naturally insulated and heated. Plants and greenery can also improve the air quality in and around your home, negating the need for air purifiers or humidifiers. There is a lot to research when it comes to minimizing utility costs through nature.

Permaculture Produces Less Waste

One of the core principles of permaculture is to make the best use of every possible product. As a result, there is far less waste in a permaculture endeavor. Composting, which we mentioned above, is a perfect example of that. It is used both as a fertilizer and a form of soil amendment. Water is another excellent example. Rainwater can be collected in barrels by placing them beneath a downspout; this, in turn, can be used to irrigate crops or attract animals. This saves on the cost of the water and is advantageous because rainwater is more nutritious and lacks all the chemical additives of tap water.

Permaculture Uses Fewer Chemicals

Permaculture uses naturally recycled garden waste for fertilizer and mulching needs. As a result, there is no need to rely on potentially harmful chemical fertilizers that cause problems when ingested with food. Instead, natural predators from your permaculture ecosystem will perform the bulk of the pest removal for you. This is because water will attract certain insects, frogs, and other wildlife which will feed on unwanted critters in your garden. The practice of companion planting will help keep most pest problems under control.

Permaculture Produces Less Pollution

Because permaculture aims to be an entirely natural undertaking, it produces little or no pollution. It operates primarily by recycling natural waste into your little self-contained ecosystem. Plant life will, to a certain extent, even help clean the air. You can also add in the lack of transportation. When you grow your own food, there is no need for more food to be shipped across the city, country, or planet.

Permaculture Helps Develop Community Values

When you adopt the permaculture philosophy and apply its principles, you will create little to no pollution, you will use only as many resources as you need, and you will give back to people, animals, and the environment. Looking after the planet starts with engaging with your community, which can be naturally accomplished through permaculture.

Permaculture Helps Manage Your Time through Zones

A zone is a fairly easy concept to understand. It's a subregion of your ecosystem in which a particular animal, plant, or group is cultivated. For example, if you have a chicken coop, the chicken coop would be its own zone. Similarly, if you have an herb garden, that herb garden might be its own zone. The point of zoning is that it helps you organize your entire permaculture ecosystem according to when and how often each component in a zone must be attended to (harvested, fertilized, etc.). Those components which require the most attention are placed nearest to your home. Those components which require the least attention are placed farthest away. By starting at your home and working your way out, you limit wasted time, both in time spent going from your home to a part of your garden and the time spent moving from one area to another.

Permaculture Supports Self Reliance and Diversity

This is actually two benefits, not one—but they are related. When you grow produce and other things in your own garden, you become naturally self-reliant. Permaculture is a guide that can help you to produce everything that you need, and this self-reliance gives you an independence you will not have had before.

Besides helping you be self-reliant, diversity also improves your permaculture ecosystem's resilience. If you have a diverse system, there is a good chance that different parts of it satisfy the same functions as other parts. So, if one part fails, you can use another part as a backup. The easiest example of this is food. If your tomatoes fail one year, maybe you'll just eat more red bell peppers instead.

Permaculture Allows a Greener Lifestyle

Permaculture is very nature-oriented and provides an environmentally friendly lifestyle. It uses natural pesticides and natural fertilizers in its care of gardens and tries to use mostly freshwater reserves like rain and natural waterways.

Permaculture aims at a "zero-waste" goal, and it can significantly reduce one's carbon footprint, even in cities. Even in an urban area, you can fully embrace a permaculture lifestyle, doing things such as recycling food waste as compost for your plants. This will help supply them with additional nitrogen, carbon, and even calcium.

In non-urban settings, the greener aspects are even more abundant. Permaculture can reduce and sometimes even reverse several agricultural problems. These include increased pesticide resistance (since you don't use them), topsoil depletion, deforestation, groundwater contamination, endangered plant species, endangered animal species, and poor social or economic conditions. It can even positively affect things as far-reaching as global warming and climate change.

Permaculture Helps Improve the Environment

A permaculture lifestyle does not harm the environment, and that alone distinguishes it from most modern farming. And, with care and effort, it can go beyond that and actually improve the environment.

One technique at permaculture's disposal is regenerative agriculture. Regenerative agriculture is concerned with rebuilding damaged farmland. Experts estimate that we are losing about 1 percent of our topsoil every year to erosion and the destruction tied to modern agriculture (www.draxe.com). Topsoil is home to untold trillions of beneficial microorganisms essential for the growth of plants, flowers, trees, and more. Without topsoil, we can't grow as much of our food. Consistently losing it year after year is a catastrophe in the making. Regenerative agriculture can reverse this loss and improve the general organic matter in the soil (not just topsoil) and improve the ground's capacity to hold water.

The point of a permaculture system is to mimic an entire ecosystem on a smaller scale. It does this by working with nature, not against it. It doesn't use artificial means like sprinkler systems or synthetic chemicals. It embraces a whole mindset that includes and supports efforts like recycling and repairing resources to limit waste, maintain species' diversity, create resilience to environmental change, and adapt to environmental change.

Permaculture Can Be Used in Older Systems

A non-permaculture agricultural system can be modified with a little care and preparation so that permaculture elements can be added to it. In some cases, it might be possible to transform the entire system, but there can be some limitations. If most of the ecological systems have been destroyed, permaculture success may be limited. This will most likely occur in locations that have seen a high degree of commercial development. It might not be hopeless, but it definitely makes things harder.

Permaculture Can Influence Insect Populations to Your Benefit

You might not realize this, but the number and type of plants you grow can influence the insects you will attract to your property. Consider perennials. Permaculture stresses the importance of using perennials because they save labor, do less damage to the soil, and will likely produce more food in the long run. It is also true that many insect populations are attracted to perennials. Bees, for example, love the rich nectar they extract from perennial flowers. In the process, they will happily pollinate your plants for you.

Of course, not all insects are as helpful as bees. Do you find mosquitos annoying? Many people do. There are several plants that mosquitos hate and avoid, like lemongrass. If you plant sufficient quantities of lemongrass on your permaculture site, you can significantly reduce mosquito problems.

Lemongrass

Permaculture Gardens Have Multiple Uses

This is the embodiment of one of the permaculture principles, the notion that you should get as much out of your garden as you can. Some people grow gardens because they look pretty. Some people grow gardens to provide food. Others grow gardens to provide natural medicines. A permaculture enthusiast grows a garden for all three of these reasons and many more. These include the production of crafting materials, developing wildlife habitat, and even just using it as a meditation space. All of these are perfect reasons to have a garden. And permaculture strives to fulfill all these functions in one space.

Permaculture Gardens Can Be Small and Convenient

The key to permaculture success is to think long-term. When building your garden, start small and work to produce sustainable yields to which you can add. Once you get going, you can rein in the growth to whatever level makes you comfortable. There is no need to overdo it. And if you are working with limited space or just want the garden to be small and compact, you have a few options to help.

Raised beds take up no more horizontal space than in-ground garden beds, but they are often very attractive, they drain quite easily, and the plants can be accessed with ease.

Likewise, in permaculture, another strategy is to use vertical gardening techniques. You can grow your plants in hanging baskets, on trellises, or even on a sturdy tree. Of course, once you get going, you can scale up your space as much as you wish. Permaculture gardens can fit any space you can imagine.

Permaculture Gardens Provide Creative and Artistic Expression

Gardening can be a highly creative art form, and permaculture can be an extremely creative form of gardening that incorporates both your mind and your sense of aesthetics. One principle of permaculture involves the use of edges. The edges between areas are highly productive because it is where a variety of different forms of life meet. Making artistic patterns throughout your garden can increase the number and size of your edges, allowing for this process to take place on a larger scale.

One type of garden bed that incorporates this principle is the keyhole garden. It is both beautiful and highly productive. It can be adapted to virtually any gardener. Keyhole gardens are usually horseshoe in shape. This allows the gardener to walk into the center and have easy access to the entire growing area.

Permaculture Gardens Are Easy to Maintain

Permaculture gardens, once they are set up and established, are very easy to maintain. The most important work is the planning that goes into it beforehand. According to gardeningknowhow.com, "Once a permaculture garden has established itself, you do nothing but water and harvest crops or add occasional mulch. Permaculture simply refers to a garden that can essentially take care of itself."

You can also design the shape of the garden with maintenance in mind. You can set up multiple garden beds near the home or, as mentioned earlier, decorate your yard with one or more keyhole gardens. Some people arrange several keyhole gardens in a circle where each one is easily accessed from the circle's center. Or, if preferred, the center of the circle might be used as another zone by planting a small tree there or establishing a small pond or other feature.

The key is harmony. Larger foliage is planted to shade other growth, and weeds are not seen as something to remove; instead, they can provide ground cover to retain moisture in the soil. If you trim bushes or trees, you can leave the cuttings where they lay to be absorbed eventually back into the soil. Even from this, you can imagine how much time is saved on fertilization and watering alone.

As can be seen, a permaculture garden is more eco-friendly, easier to maintain, serves multiple functions, produces more nutritious crops, is more sustainable, and adds natural beauty to your property.

Chapter 4: Designing the Space

The first step in your permaculture journey is the design phase. This is a critical step that should neither be skipped nor brief. It is essential to your success as a permaculture enthusiast to invest thoroughly in your vision. According to Permaculture News, "Permaculture design is essentially a multi-faceted, integrated, and ecologically harmonious method of designing human-centered landscapes."

In other words, permaculture design seeks to create systems that can sustain both human life and nature. This is done in an integrated fashion so that each element works in harmony with the others. As a result, the outputs from one element may be used as inputs for another element, often creating miniature closed loops within a closed system. The result is a reduction in waste, an increase in resilience, and an increase in efficiency.

Essentials of Permaculture Design

Several different elements are involved in permaculture design. Five of the most important are: Mainframe Design, Sector Analysis, Zone Planning, Workflows or Lifeflows, and The Relationships between Components.

Mainframe Design

The mainframe refers to the major features that are present in the average permaculture area. Discussions of mainframe design involve water, access, and physical structures. All of these are important, and their consideration is necessary to the success of the garden.

Water

Since water is necessary for life, it is a critical element of a permaculture establishment. Your gardens will require water. Your animals (including wildlife) will require water. And you will require water.

A critical factor of water management on a permaculture site is the understanding that the journey of water is cyclical. It will pass through your site eventually, no matter what you do to it or how you interact with it. Permaculture design tries to maximize the number of interactions with it on-site to maximize the use of every drop. Eventually, it will cycle out of the site, but only after having been used to the fullest possible extent.

There are three aspects to the permaculture approach to water: slow, spread, and sink.

Slowing water generally refers to its capture and storage either in tanks or on-site ponds.

Spreading of water refers to how it is used on-site—to nourish crops, feed animals, etc. Spreading water may involve using and mapping topological features like the contours and general slope of the land.

The sinking of water involves the release of water back into nature. Water can be directed to exit the permaculture site, or allowed to take its own path back into the environment. An example of this could be an irrigation system that allows water to hydrate the roots of plants and then drains the excess into a waterway instead of diverting it into a storm-drain or simply leaving it to evaporate.

Access

Access is how you get into and around your site.

The more secluded the location of your permaculture site, the more essential a path will be to reach it. You can't build on the top of a mountain and expect getting there to be easy. If you build it far from where you live, you will disturb the natural environment if you have to walk through it or build a pathway.

Constructing roads is an expensive proposition, but there are a few rules of thumb:

1. If possible, try to cross a valley on a dam or pond wall.

2. Follow the contours of the land as much as you can.

3. Use ridge lines to ascend and descend.

The point of these rules is to help spare the environment from unnecessary erosion due to accommodating the increased traffic flow. You want to build the path in a location the water flows away from, not one the water flows towards; otherwise, it will be exposed to more flowing water and erode faster.

Roads and paths aren't the only consideration when it comes to access. It also refers to how you move about your site. Fences and gates fall under this heading. Even something like a keyhole garden, which allows the person in the center to reach every edge of the garden easily, would fall into this category.

If you do not need to build a path or road, do not build one, but if you must, then ensure that you are disturbing the natural environment as little as possible when you are moving through the space.

Physical Structures: Space Use, Buildings, etc.

The last point to consider under mainframe design is the nature of the actual structures on your site. These structures can include greenhouses, gardens, solar panels, a water collection system, and much more. Each item will have its own size, benefits, and particular needs.

A house, for example, must be of sufficient size to support the family that lives there. It must have sufficient methods of access, both to the outside world (through intelligent use of roads, etc.) and to the products of the site, be they food, water, or other needs. Smart mainframe design can lead to increases in efficiency and prevent future problems.

For example, consider the idea of building a house on a hill. Not only will road construction be a problem, but you may also have issues getting water to the site. If the water must come from the bottom of the hill, you'll need some sort of power source or pressure source to transport it up to your home. Similarly, you probably don't want to place the home too far away from the permaculture site, making half of your lengthy trips to it uphill. Finally, there are climate and weather considerations; any house needs to remain warm in the winter and cool in the summer. This usually becomes a bigger issue on hilltops due to the increased exposure to the elements, though strategically placed trees can provide shade in the winter, while proper insulation combined with windows placed to take maximum advantage of the winter sun can help heat the home during the cold months.

Another structure to consider is the permaculture garden itself. One of the principles of permaculture design is the minimizing of space used on site. Permaculture gardens are meant to provide large amounts of products from economical use of space. One technique that allows this is called stacking. Permaculture embraces the idea that more than one crop can be grown in the same space. Carrots and onions grow well together, for example, as do corn, beans, and cucumbers. In the latter example, the corn provides a vertical stalk for the beans to climb, the beans pull up nutrients from deeper in the soil, and the cucumbers sprawl across the ground, protecting it from damage and helping retain water. The products work together for mutual benefit. So, instead of growing one crop in a designated space, you can grow multiple crops simultaneously. This kind of approach can, even in urban areas, allow one to stack plants on a balcony or rooftop and incorporate a permaculture lifestyle in a small space.

Those are just two examples of permaculture structures-planning that create extra benefits from thoughtful planning before implementation.

Sector Analysis

Sector analysis deals with studying and observing the various natural forces and energies that affect your site. This can include sunlight, seasonal winds, rain, regular flooding, animal migration, and other recurring natural phenomena. They are unavoidable and not controlled by any human activity or any on-site design. They come from outside. But, since they occur regularly, reactions to their presence can be built into the design.

A good example of this is sunlight. In the northern hemisphere, the sun sits lower in the southern portion of the sky during winter and higher during summer. This can influence the placement of windows for winter months, shade trees for the summer, and the garden's general location and orientation. Depending on how far north you are, you will probably place the garden on the south side of the house to gain more sunlight.

The intensity of the sun will also dictate the type of produce that you can grow. There is a reason why some crops can only be grown in warmer climates, and there are also great options for growing in cooler climates. You cannot start your permaculture design thinking that you are going to be able to grow anything that you want. Before deciding on the type of garden you are going to utilize, you should thoroughly research what can be grown in your climate. One thing to also keep in mind is that just because a certain crop is not *usually* grown in your climate, it does not mean that it *cannot* be grown. Often, crops are not grown because the soil lacks the right nutrients or there is not enough shade. With permaculture design, you *can* grow crops that are generally not grown in your area.

Once you develop a plan to maximize the use of sunlight, you can move on to other energies. Another such force of nature is the wind. Trees and buildings can be used as windbreakers. This can help shield delicate plants in a garden from damage or even shield the main home from blasts of cold winter air. In breezy or windy locales, windmills can pump water, produce electricity, and power mechanical devices.

Zones

Zones are another aspect of permaculture design, and they should not be confused with sectors. Where sectors are arranged according to the presence of natural forces you can't control, zones are all about the things you can control. According to Permaculture News, "Zoning is simply a design process that we use to spatially place elements within our system relative to our center of attention as determined by their energy and maintenance requirements." There are six different zones in a permaculture design, numbered 0 through 5.

- **Zone 0:** This is the central structure of the home. This is your living space and the center of your whole permaculture endeavor. This zone includes things that are grown within your home and could also include herb gardens in windowsill boxes.

- **Zone 1:** This is where the most intensive and productive gardens are placed, such as fruits and vegetables. You also want to think about how often you will visit the zones. As Zone 1 is the area surrounding your home, you will visit it more often. If herbs are not grown in your home, it makes sense to have them in zone 1 as you will often be visiting your herb garden. When it comes to fruit trees, it might make sense to plant fruit trees here if you will harvest some fruit daily, though for larger fruit crops that will be harvested all at once, a zone farther from the house is recommended.

- **Zone 2:** This is a less intensive zone, which might include chicken coops and less-visited kitchen gardens. It may include food forests, milking sheds for dairy animals, and even something like a duck pond.

- **Zone 3:** This is for more large-scale productions like crops of corn, potatoes, and grains, as well as pasture for various grazing animals. The things here require less attention than zones 0, 1, and 2, but they are still close enough that you can feed animals as needed and be able to tend your crops.

- **Zone 4:** Very little effort is required here. This is where things like trees planted for timber or firewood are found, or permanent pastures for grazing animals. Generally, they require little visitation and are mostly self-sufficient (it is worth noting that just because these things are in the outer zones, it does not mean that you won't visit them regularly. They are still part of your permaculture site, and you may enjoy walking with the animals even if you are not there to tend to them).

- **Zone 5:** This is the wilderness zone. It is used primarily for observation, learning, and meditation. You come here to study nature on its own terms. What you learn here can be applied to your other zones. Zone 5 may include an area such as a forest that you walk within but do not try to change.

Not all of these zones may be needed or used. Zones four and five are definitely optional, and some people, particularly city-dwellers, may get away with just a zone zero and a zone one. What you need to do, though, is to figure your zones in advance. And also, note that the zones themselves are not hard and fast delineations. They are just to give you a general idea and get you thinking about how to plan your site. What you should keep foremost in your mind are the relationships between the different zones and their constituent parts and, even more importantly, their relationships with your habitation area. For example, you may place the chicken coop in Zone 2 and use the resulting manure to help fertilize the gardens in Zone 1. This creates a relationship between those two zones that is important to keep in mind while planning. Similarly, the gardens in Zone 1, since they generate produce that you frequently consume, have a relationship with Zone 0, your home.

Workflows or Lifeflows

Workflows or lifeflows is another area of permaculture design. It is the process of taking the patterns of human life into account with respect to your design. For example, it might deal with where you place your tool shed. If you place it in an area that is hard to get to, you'll likely wind up with lost and abandoned tools because putting the tools back where they belong becomes annoyingly inconvenient.

You can use the concept to design daily routines. You might set your site up such that all your morning stops are on the same path (chicken coop, vegetable garden, etc.), and the same for your evening routine. The idea is to make life comfortable, not awkward.

A simple example might be planting your tomatoes near your herb garden. Now, when you come to pick your tomato and a few basil leaves for lunch, you only have to visit one place.

The Relationships between Components

You want to connect as many components as you can in as many ways as possible and build redundancies so that the entire site is more resilient. That way, if something happens to one component, another component can step in and take over the first component's role. For example, if your tomatoes fail, perhaps you can substitute red peppers or some other vegetable.

When planning this, you must analyze each component and break it down into intrinsic characteristics, needs, products, and behaviors.

This kind of analysis is essential, particularly when it comes to planning out stacked gardens. Stacked gardens, as mentioned earlier, conserve space by growing multiple plants in the same area. This is possible when you use companion gardening or guilds (multiple plants that work well together). You want to stack plants that work well together, like the previously mentioned carrots and onions or the three sisters of corn, beans, and cucumbers (or, for example, squash).

As noted above, the corn provides the climbing medium for the beans; the beans, in turn, pull up nutrients from the soil, and the cucumbers or squash will serve to shield and preserve the soil for the benefit of all three. This demonstrates stacking, and how the outputs of some elements can serve as inputs for other elements, thus creating a harmonious design. An alternative to stacked gardening in space is stack gardening in time. Here, you plant foods that will ripen at different times. That way, you will always be getting food from the garden, but the type will vary depending upon the season.

Permaculture design is an extensive subject with a lot of details within its various elements. That's because the field of permaculture is immense and varied, ranging across a vast number of scientific disciplines as well as thoughtful, ethical philosophies. The lesson here, though, is to prepare and plan in advance, thinking big but starting small.

Chapter 5: Permaculture in Urban Areas

Permaculture offers a great way to become more self-sufficient. It allows you to reduce your carbon footprint and overall impact on the environment and the planet's natural systems. However, what if you live in an *un*natural ecosystem, like a city? At first glance, permaculture may appear to be incompatible with an urban lifestyle. But this is far from the truth.

Although it may not be possible for you totally to eliminate your environmental footprint if you live in a city, you can certainly reduce it considerably. Permaculture provides several methods and techniques along with a whole new mindset that will help you in this journey.

Gardening Locations for Small Spaces

In a city environment, one of your primary gardening concerns is a lack of space. However, even if you live in a single-room efficiency, you have options. You just have to do a little research and, perhaps, a little out-of-the-box thinking. Consider these possibilities: windows, balconies, rooftops, community gardens, and land share.

Windows

Many people in cities live in apartments with a bathroom, a bedroom, a kitchen, and if they're lucky, a small living room. That's not much space in which to build a garden. But most apartments have windows that let in sunlight and heat; you can capture this energy and use it to grow a window garden. You can go the traditional route and grow a few herbs or some simple fruits and vegetables, such as tomatoes and lettuce, in a window box. Alternatively, you can get creative and use plastic bottles to take advantage of the vertical space on the window. Plastic bottles are light and durable, so they make excellent plant containers that can be strung together from the top of the window to the bottom. This makes excellent use of plastic (the man-made bane of the environment), keeping it from taking up space in a landfill. Another option is to grow mushrooms from a mushroom kit in a dark, secluded area of the apartment. You can also grow live cultures for yogurt, sourdough, or anything else that requires "starter" or live cultures.

Balconies

Many city apartments have balconies that can be used for growing container gardens. Of course, they have to be situated properly, and you should do the same kind of permaculture analysis that you would for any other site. You need to consider and determine things like what areas receive most of the sunlight, what areas are shaded, how much rainfall do the different areas get, and the wind patterns. Another important point to consider is soil needs. If your balcony is reasonably close to your kitchen, you can easily adapt the permaculture practice of composting and amend the soil in the pots with kitchen scraps, or even take up worm farming. Finally, when growing plants on your balcony, don't forget you have vertical space available. Installing a trellis or similar tall structure that vines can climb is not difficult.

Rooftops

A rooftop is a great place to grow plants in the city. However, if you don't own the roof and have access to it, you'll need to get permission. Also, you will need to make sure that the building is strong enough to support the extra weight of a rooftop garden. Provided you protect your garden from strong winds, you should be met with great success if you focus on plants that thrive in direct sunlight, such as lettuce, tomatoes, sweet corn, and eggplant. Also, a good addition to such a garden is a rooftop beehive. Bees adapt reasonably well to city life, particularly when housed near a garden where they can find food and assist in pollination.

Community Gardens

Another option for the city dweller is to seek out and make use of community gardens. Some cities and towns have turned unused land into viable gardens for growing food. You can inquire at your local council office to find about such options in your area. If there isn't one, perhaps you can get one started.

Land Share

One more option for city residents interested in permaculture is land share. In this situation, you need to find someone who has land you can use. You can offer to set up, build, and maintain a garden on their land and split the produce with them, or you can rent the land from them and keep all of the produce. They have the land but lack the time or motivation, while you have the motivation but don't have space. Just be sure to come to an arrangement before you get started.

Even in a city, you may have access to several potential permaculture spaces. The key is to think outside the box. Get creative about it and believe in yourself.

Gardening Techniques for Small Places

Besides being creative about what you set aside as a space to grow a garden (a balcony, rooftop, community garden, etc.), you can also get creative regarding the different techniques and methods you use to grow your garden. Permaculture has a number of specialized techniques designed specifically for small spaces like those found in urban settings. Here are just a few: vertical gardens, container gardens, curbside gardens, keyhole garden beds, and square-foot gardening.

Vertical Gardens

A vertical garden is exactly what it sounds like: a garden that uses vertical space instead of horizontal space. You may be limited by your reach and the space available, but vertical gardens provide an excellent method to give your plants maximum exposure to sunlight while conserving space. A common example of a vertical garden is one grown on a trellis (a lattice-work of intersecting wood or metal planks that provide a vertical growing surface for climbing plants and trees). A trellis provides an excellent surface for the vines of a climbing plant to wrap around, grab on to, and get more sun. A trellis can also provide shade and protect other plants from the sun.

Another method of vertical gardening is called "espalier". This technique involves pruning and shaping a woody plant, like an apple tree, so that it will grow up against a wall or fence. Again, this preserves space by keeping the plant pressed against the wall or fence and is considered vertical gardening because it conserves space (and the fact that growth is mainly upward).

Container Gardens

Container gardens are one of the most traditional space-conserving garden methods used in the West. They consist of a collection of containers or pots, each growing one or several types of plants. If you are using permaculture techniques, it will probably be several plants that meet the criteria for companion planting. Also, the type of container may show permaculture influences, particularly if you decide to extend the useful life of a plastic container you acquired for other purposes. For example, a plastic juice bottle can be readily transformed into a serviceable plant container. Doing so saves you the money you might have spent purchasing a store-bought plant container and keeps that bottle from a landfill.

Curbside Gardens

A curbside garden or median strip garden is planted in the space found between a street and a sidewalk. This is usually considered public land, so you will likely need local council or government permission. Most are reasonable when it comes to utilizing spaces in this way, so you shouldn't have much difficulty getting permission. Plants, flowers, herbs, and even fruit trees have been known to thrive in such spaces. They add to the city's greenery, help the local population with food, and even improve the local air quality.

Keyhole Garden Beds

Keyhole garden beds provide an excellent way to use space. Since the price of land in an urban area is usually much higher than land in a rural area, if you are lucky enough to have some land in a city, it is likely a very small plot. But keyhole gardens can fit comfortably in a small plot of land. They maximize the use of growing space within their confines because every square inch can be used. The only "path" in a keyhole garden is the ingress/egress and small empty area near the center that lets you reach every part of the garden.

Square-Foot Gardening

Square-foot gardening is another gardening system designed to maximize the output of a small area. It is a form of intensive gardening where the gardening area is broken down into smaller one-foot-by-one-foot squares. Normal square-foot gardens consist of a four-foot-by-four-foot plot of land divided in such a fashion. This gives you a total of sixteen squares in which to work. Typically, a square-foot garden is placed in a raised bed, making it easy to access.

These gardening techniques will help you as you pursue your permaculture goals to overcome your deficiency in space. Remember to keep an eye on the big picture but take baby steps to begin.

The Art of Composting

If you have never composted before, track how much organic material you throw out regularly. You might be surprised at how much of your garbage is actually useable organic material. Recognize that this waste, when thrown out, usually winds up in a landfill where it does little environmental good. There is a much better use for all that material; *composting.*

What is Composting, and What Does It Do?

Composting is a method of recycling organic material back into the environment to add nutrients and organic matter to the soil, as opposed to the usual alternative which is to waste such material by sending it to a landfill. At the landfill, all it will really do is help increase methane emissions which contribute to global warming. With composting, you collect your organic waste such as leftover food scraps, food waste, and even twice-read newspapers or old books, throw them together into a composting bin, and out pops nourishment for your soil. This is added to your garden, increasing your soil's access to nutrients and, ultimately, increasing your garden's yield.

What Do You Compost?

Composting involves the recycling of organic matter. But some types of organic matter are better than others. The particulars will vary from kitchen to kitchen depending upon what each person regularly consumes. Bread, cereal, coffee grounds, eggshells, fruits, grains, tea bags, and vegetables are all standard composting materials, and you can even sprinkle eggshells and coffee grinds straight on your soil. Both will add nutrients, with coffee grinds giving you additional nitrogen and phosphorous, and eggshells are a great pest deterrent. Meat, fish, fatty and oily foods, dairy products, and bones can be harder to compost and may attract pests if not done right, so research composting before undertaking it if you are throwing these things out.

Composting in a City

If you live in a city, you may not have room for a normal compost bin. Even if you do, you may not put the bin to full use because it may be too large for the amount of compost you need for your garden. There may be an issue with odor or attracting pests depending upon what you are trying to compost (see above). There is, however, a handy solution to your problems. It's called vermicomposting.

Vermicomposting

This is a composting method that uses worms to produce compost. It can be used inside or outside, but your interest will likely be to learn about using it inside if you live in a city. You collect organic matter and store it in a container (even a plastic one!) about the size of a shoebox, with a tight-fitting lid. Drill holes in the upper sides and the lid, layer the bottom with wetted newspaper and drop in a couple of hundred worms (red wigglers are preferred). Next, add in the organic material, cover everything with newspaper strips, and replace the lid. Remove the lid if the container ever fogs up. Gauge how much food the worms eat by checking every couple of days.

If vermicomposting is not your thing, you can also contact your local authority and see if they have a composting system. Many cities and towns collect all your green waste and then compost it at a large facility. The compost is often available to the public, and you can pick some up at your leisure.

Composting goes back to Principle Two of permaculture, "Catching and Storing Energy." In this case, the energy is found in organic matter. You catch that energy by saving the organic waste, letting it turn into compost, and adding the compost to your garden. It's a permaculture principle at work.

Although by themselves, the above techniques and methods probably won't make you entirely self-sufficient if you live in a city, they will help you reduce your environmental footprint, and that is a victory in itself as far as the permaculture lifestyle is concerned.

Chapter 6: Permaculture Gardening

Many people are interested in the permaculture movement, but many don't realize that the term "permaculture" really embraces more than just gardening techniques. In reality, it embraces a whole philosophy and way of life. In its broadest sense, permaculture incorporates things like renewable energy, sustainable housing, cyclical systems, and even, to a certain extent, the inner workings of small communities. The first step people take who get involved in permaculture, however, usually comes through gardening.

A permaculture garden is a journey on its own. It provides an excellent first step into the broader world of permaculture as a whole. A permaculture garden differs from a regular garden in many respects. It is even substantially different from an organic garden, although both the permaculture garden and the organic garden share an interest in and a concern for environmental issues.

What Is a Permaculture Garden and What Does It Need?

A permaculture garden is a garden that incorporates the three ethical tenets of permaculture as well as the twelve principles. It begins with observation, study, and planning. It proceeds by using the existing features of the landscape and carefully enhancing them where appropriate to build an environmentally conscious, highly productive garden of sufficient size for your time and needs.

You start building your garden on the macro-level and progressively becoming more and more granular (Principle #7: Design from Pattern to Details). First, you place the garden and its constituent parts according to the needs of your particular area. You might make use of the natural contours of your land or dig swales. From there, you design the features over the garden by adding in garden beds, water systems, and whatever else other infrastructure might be required. Finally, you begin planting, starting with perennials and then adding annuals.

In general, you try to work with natural forces to make the task of building and maintaining your garden easier. That is, you study the wind, the rain, and the sun to optimize their effects on your garden. This will, in turn, help reduce your labor by harnessing nature to provide the food, water, shelter, and whatever else your garden might need besides seeds and plants.

As you build your permaculture garden, you may reflect on and compare it to traditional gardens. Although both strategies share the same fundamental goal—to provide food—they differ in many important respects.

How a Permaculture Garden Differs From a Traditional Garden

A permaculture garden invests more labor in pre-planning, thought, and strategizing than a traditional garden does.

Beyond that, the permaculture garden differs in these areas: treatment of soil, the use of perennials, mulching strategies, space utilization, and the virtual elimination of waste.

Treatment of Soil

A permaculture garden differs from a traditional garden in how it treats the soil. First and foremost, a permaculture garden looks at soil as something to be built up and grown rather than simply supporting the plants we consume. It begins with the ideas of one-dig and no-till garden beds. Tilling and digging up soil is actually harmful to it, killing many of the beneficial microorganisms that normally call it home, destroying a host of beneficial nutrients, and slowly, inevitably, wearing the topsoil away. Because permaculture avoids such practices and, instead, actively seeks to build the soil up, a permaculture garden can become more productive over time instead of exhausting the soil and ruining the land, as can happen with traditional gardens.

With the permaculture approach, you have a number of methods to help you preserve your soil. The strategic use of mulch and ground cover crops will help keep the soil in place and protect it from heavy rain or intense sunlight. Well-crafted garden beds that allow access to their entire area without the necessity of setting foot in them (e.g., keyhole gardens) will keep the soil from being compacted by heavy footfalls. This will allow air and water to permeate the soil with relative ease, much to its benefit.

Use of Perennials

Perennials are another important feature of permaculture gardens that most traditional gardens lack. Perennial plants live longer than annuals, sometimes having lifespans of three years, five years, or even longer. In fact, perennials, because of their longevity and inculcation into the most well-balanced ecosystems, represent one of the most critical distinguishing features of permaculture gardens. That is, few if any traditional gardens form a mutually intertwined ecosystem by themselves. Permaculture gardens do or are designed to do so to whatever extent they can. Because of that, the permaculture garden requires less effort to maintain and will be naturally more productive. Of course, our diet has been focused mostly on annuals for a very long time. Shifting our diets to perennials is likely to take some effort. Appropriate plants to start with include various berries, nuts, garlic, kale, rhubarb, and more.

Mulching Strategies: Another critical aspect of permaculture gardening is the use of mulch. This goes hand and hand with the treatment of the soil, as mentioned above. Mulching does many things. For example:

- It adds nutrients to the soil.

- It reduces the growth of weeds, meaning less weeding for you.

- It helps prevent the soil from drying out by locking moisture in, thereby keeping the moisture for the plants.

- It stops the soil from eroding or compacting too tightly.

- It provides a habitat for worms, insects, microorganisms, and other living things that improve the soil.

- It helps build multiple layers of fresh, new soil.

One particular type of mulching that is often used in permaculture gardens deserves special mention. It is called sheet mulching or "lasagna gardening." It involves alternately layering different materials in sequence, such as compost, cardboard, leaves, straw, wood chips, and other materials, one atop the other. Thus, you are forming a series of layers that look like a slice of lasagna if a cross-section were observed. However, keep in mind that sheet mulching usually takes a bit of time to decompose, so it is usually best done in the fall before the spring in which you begin planting.

Utilization of Space

As discussed in the preceding chapter, the use of space is one feature of permaculture gardens that allows their development in urban settings. However, you should know that maximizing the use of space is not something permaculture does only in cities. Rural permaculture gardens also seek to maximize the use of space. Multiple plants of different types are often grown intertwined with each other in compact garden beds. These are usually more visually stimulating than row upon row of the same plants being grown together across the entire length of a normal garden plot. The traditional garden seems somehow sterile and artificial in comparison. Too controlled. Too rigid. As PermacultureNews says, "The unnatural world has taught us to overvalue the straight line. It works well for building houses quickly or getting from point A to B fastest, but curves—both along the sides and vertical throughout the bed—make more surface area and microclimates for plants."

Traditional gardens may be productive, but they are hardly natural in either appearance or implementation. Plus, keeping them neat and orderly, their rows distinct, separate, and navigable requires an enormous amount of labor that is not needed in a permaculture garden.

Elimination of Waste

One of the primary goals, and a critical defining feature, of permaculture gardens, is that they create virtually no waste. Basically, everything grown in the garden is either eaten or returned to the garden as compost or mulch or something else. If plants die without producing anything, they are simply returned to the system. If leaves fall, they are returned to the system. Weeds, trimmings, and everything else is returned to the system. You must look at your garden as a complete ecosystem with cycles. Plants can be grown simply to harvest the seeds. Legumes can be grown and turned into mulch to boost nitrogen in the soil. Never remove anything from the system if it can be helped. Never throw anything out. That is the key to sustainability. The goal is to develop your garden and your gardening practices so that the whole system becomes self-sustaining. Not only is that a financial boon, but it is an environmentally sound goal as well.

How a Permaculture Garden Differs from an Organic Garden

Permaculture gardens and organic gardens spring from the same source: an awareness that humanity's environmental practices need to change. Both disciplines realize that how we treat the Earth when we garden and grow food must not undermine the health and longevity of our environment. Both have the same goal: sustainable food production.

The difference is, though, that permaculture involves a more all-encompassing philosophy and lifestyle. It is the next logical step in greener living after organic gardening. Neither one wants to use fertilizers or pesticides, many of the modern synthetic chemicals damaging our environment and water systems. Both might incorporate companion planting as a natural method to replace those dangerous pesticides and fertilizers.

The primary difference is that permaculture recognizes that your entire garden can and should be treated as its own entire ecosystem. An organic garden may resemble a traditional garden. For example, nothing says that an organic garden cannot exist with a whole slew of boring rows of the same plant growing side by side in one gigantic plot. Similarly, organic does not have the same emphasis put on self-sustainability that permaculture does. There is nothing wrong with importing new seeds of the same produce every year or purchasing the same natural fertilizer yearly. An organic garden can reach beyond itself to find its needs. Ideally, other than at start-up time, a permaculture garden does not.

The permaculture garden seeks to emulate nature more thoroughly than an organic garden by setting itself up as, and treating itself as, an entire self-contained ecosystem. The primary characteristic that makes that possible is self-sustainability.

Permaculture Gardens Are Self-Sustaining

This was mentioned above in the discussion of traditional gardens, but it also applies when comparing permaculture gardens to organic gardens. A self-sustaining garden meets three needs: no yearly purchasing, excess garden outputs are used as inputs, and soil must be continuously rebuilt to produce an effective yield.

• **No Yearly Purchasing:** This involves getting all garden supplies from on-site. This includes things like seeds. Normally, as in an organic garden, you have the option of purchasing organic seeds from someplace off-site to bring back and grow in your garden. Other than at start-up, permaculture gardens do not do this. If you want more seeds of a particular type, you can grow a few extra plants and harvest their seeds. The same principle holds true for natural fertilizers and anything else that your permaculture garden needs. They should all be generated on-site.

• **Excess Garden Outputs:** Again, this was touched on in the discussion of traditional gardens but is mentioned here in the discussion of organic gardens too. In a permaculture garden, nothing is ever wasted, thrown away, or carted away. That is not necessarily true of organic gardens.

• **Soil Is Rebuilt:** This is actually true of any type of garden that intends to produce a yield for more than just a few seasons. What distinguishes the permaculture garden in this respect is how it is done: by using on-site resources. Many traditional or organic gardens will add new soil from off-site every year.

The last thing that should be mentioned is that there is some overlap between the concepts of organic gardens and permaculture gardens. Whereas not all organic gardens qualify as permaculture, and, if the truth be known, not all permaculture gardens strictly qualify as organic gardens (they might break a small rule here or there), many gardens qualify as both.

The Difference between Annuals and Perennials

There are three basic types of flowering plants: annuals, perennials, and biennials. Annuals complete their entire life cycle in a single season. Perennials take several seasons. Biennials share characteristics of both. Carrots, for example, are a biennial plant with a life cycle of two years.

All three of these types of plants have a place in permaculture gardening. Neither annuals or perennials are superior to each other, which is something you should keep in mind when comparing the two. If you want the best of both worlds, integrate them together into your garden design. You'll have an unlimited option in terms of form, color, texture and blooming time. This is a perfect example of embracing three of permaculture's principles: 8) Integrate, don't segregate, 10) Use and value diversity, and 11) Use edges and value the marginal. By its very nature, integrating involves mixing plants of different types like perennials, annuals, and biennials. Furthermore, perennials and annuals (and even biennials) exist together in nature. That is a form of diversity.

Similarly, since the end of one plant can mark the beginning of another, that can also be understood as a margin or an edge where interesting things happen. Those are not the only reasons why the plants are used together in permaculture gardens, but they are three very important ones. Additionally, the plants usually work together well aesthetically speaking. That is, they often create beautiful arrays of color and light, which can also be a significant "yield" (Principle #3) for some.

Why You Should Use Annuals

In the first few years of your garden, the perennials may be slow in developing. You'll want to have many edible annuals that can fill that gap so you can still reap a harvest even though your perennials are largely barren. You'll likely wish to keep some annuals going in your garden because they can be used to attract bees and other pollinating insects to increase the overall yield of your entire garden. And they may serve a role in one of your groups of companion plants (like with corn, beans, and squash). Last, you may find a few annuals you think are visually appealing all by themselves.

Why You Should Use Perennials

Perennials cost less over the long term because they return every year. Those savings can add up over time. They also serve as the foundation of many combinations of stacked plants, growing into fully-fledged trees that offer shade to shade-loving plants while serving as climbing posts for many vines. They also tend to use less water, if that is a concern in your region. Finally, they can help establish a habitat for local wildlife and pollinating insects.

Why You Should Use Biennials

You should use biennials for many of the same reasons that you use annuals and perennials, including variety, aesthetics, attracting wildlife, and more. Biennials are also hardy plants that grow root systems in their first year and flower in their second. One advantage of this is that they are not competing for the same nutrients as other plants and often grow later in the season. They are also hardier, so they can be planted in high-use areas while still thriving.

A good permaculture garden incorporates all these elements and ideas, from lasagna gardening to soil amending and composting to the stacking of perennials and annuals. Most importantly, permaculture is an ecological adventure, but more than that; it is an ecological adventure with a social conscience.

Chapter 7: Growing with Greenhouses

One of the challenges of living in colder climes is obtaining food in the colder months. When snow is on the ground, very little can be grown on farms or, for that matter, found in the wilderness. This need led to the development of greenhouses. Greenhouses allow you to grow food even when it gets extremely cold.

As in other areas of agriculture, permaculture gives its own twist to the concept of the greenhouse, incorporating its many principles and tenets and, if possible, making greenhouses even "greener."

What Is a Greenhouse?

The purpose of your basic greenhouse is to grow produce during the colder months. If you grow your produce in the summer and opt to buy your produce in the winter, you have to factor in the shipping of the food, along with the loss of nutrients as the food is treated and stored. That does not tie into the permaculture ethos. The solution to this issue is to grow your vegetables in a greenhouse. This removes any need for transit, cutting down the harm to the environment and delivering you food packed with nutrients and flavor.

How Do You Build a Greenhouse?

Plants need two major elements in winter that they normally do not get: light and heat. Greenhouses are designed to produce both these elements.

How Does It Work?

A greenhouse is an enclosed space whose walls and ceiling are constructed from a transparent material like glass or plastic that lets light and heat into the structure during the colder months (of course, you can also use your greenhouse in warmer months). The greenhouse will trap the heat and light inside the structure, emulating the natural conditions of the warmer months.

The rays from the sun easily pass through the transparent walls of the greenhouse, carrying with them their energy. The light strikes various objects in the greenhouse (such as plants, ponds of water, structures, or even just the ground) and transfers this energy to them through absorption. This causes the objects to heat up. Note: dark objects absorb heat more effectively than light-colored objects. As a result, a black object will absorb more heat than a white object because the white object serves to reflect light, and the black object does not. Because of this, some people may paint some items in their greenhouse black to help warm the interior. If you find yourself needing to generate more heat, this may be an option for you.

As the objects heat up, they release the heat they've acquired into the air, but more slowly than the rate at which they acquired it. This allows heat acquired during the day to be released slowly all through the day and night, retaining a consistent heat level within the greenhouse. For the heat to escape the confines of the greenhouse, the heat must transfer from the air to the glass/plastic and then outside. It does this, but not as efficiently or as quickly as the light entering the greenhouse. Essentially, light penetrates the glass or plastic easily, is absorbed into the objects within the greenhouse, and heat is released slowly, meaning a continual build-up of heat. Glass and plastic are not great insulators, but they allow for the easy transit of light.

Some greenhouses work so well they can sometimes grow too warm. This is easily solved with vents, windows, shade from trees, or even fans to help reduce the temperatures within. Of course, being a permaculture structure, we do not want to let the excess heat just disappear. If you have too much heat in your greenhouse, how can you use it? If you connect your greenhouse to a barn or shed, you can siphon off the excess heat and use it to warm other structures in the winter. Always be looking at energy outputs and how they can become inputs.

TMV

The objects in a greenhouse absorb heat and then release it slowly. Some objects release heat more slowly than others. As a result, they may serve greenhouse needs better. The measurement of this is the Thermal Mass Value or TMV. It is measured in BTU/Sq. Ft/degree F. The following table gives the values from a variety of different materials that might be useful in a greenhouse.

TMV Table*

Substance	TMV	Substance	TMV
Water	63	Brick	24
Steel	59	Sand	22
Stone	35	Earth	20
Concrete	35	Wood	10.6

The higher the TMV, the better the substance is at storing heat. So, if you can work a small pond of water into your greenhouse, that's a great idea. As is using steel supports for structures inside instead of wood—at least as far as the TMV is concerned.

What Are Its Benefits?

The most obvious benefit of a greenhouse is fresh fruits and vegetables in the months when you cannot grow them outside. But there are other advantages as well.

• A greenhouse offers a better protected and controlled environment year-round, not just in winter.

• It has potential from a business perspective as it allows you to produce fresh produce year-round. This can supply yourself, your neighbors, and others with fresh excess produce.

• It provides a growing space and a space to exercise, meditate, play in the dirt, make art, or just breathe in rich air during the winter.

• It helps maximize diversity by incorporating all the elements of a permaculture garden. Inside, you can plant a variety of different plants, stacked crops, and an established microclimate. It is as much about discovery as it is about work. Although there is always something to do, the tasks involved are varied and positive for one's health.

• It is close to your home. Permaculture design involves the use of zones, each one progressing farther and farther away from your home. Attaching a greenhouse powered by the sun to the side of your house is an excellent way to reduce your use of fossil fuels for heat. Heat can be readily exchanged as needed through a shared wall between the two structures. And, of course, accessing the food is easy and swift.

• It integrates many features into a cohesive whole. With permaculture design, the impact of every feature upon every other feature is analyzed and understood. Every aspect serves multiple functions, while at the same time, each one of those functions is accomplished by various aspects, so there is built-in redundancy.

• It embraces nature instead of fighting it. The idea is to bring a little slice of nature inside instead of using brute force to bend it to your will. Pollinating insects like bees, wasps, and butterflies inhabit the permaculture greenhouse, performing well-suited tasks. The same is true of decomposing critters like soil bacteria and earthworms.

• It is a beautiful and aesthetic creation. Humans have a need for and are naturally attuned to nature. That alone makes it a good idea to build a permaculture greenhouse. It will help you appreciate nature and life all the more by providing an oasis of fertility and energy in the dead of winter. As hobbyfarms.com states, "The permaculture greenhouse provides an ambiance where all living things thrive together."

Clearly, a permaculture greenhouse is an excellent option for anyone seeking to adopt the permaculture lifestyle.

Building a Greenhouse

There are a number of different ways to build a greenhouse and several different techniques to assist in such projects. Permaculture gardens, of course, stress a more natural approach to the endeavor, but obviously, not at the expense of the entire project. Some of the techniques that can be used include:

Storing Heat in Water: Due to its high TMV and availability, water can provide an effective means of moving heat through a greenhouse.

Glazing the Greenhouse: Glazing refers to the material covering the greenhouse and letting in light and heat. The R-value of the given substance measures it. These values can range from a decimal value to 10, 20, or even higher. The higher the number, the more heat the substance can hold in.

Soap Bubble Insulation: An interesting technique was developed by Harvey Rayner's Solar Bubble Build in the U.K. It involves using a screen of soap bubbles between two layers of polyethylene to insulate the interior.

Thermal Mass Rocket Stoves: A Thermal Mass Rocket Stove can be used to burn surplus wood to provide heat for your greenhouse. Compared to a wood stove, it is more efficient, requiring ¼ the wood, and it provides a 90% cleaner burn.

Wood Gasification: Wood gasification is the process of burning wood in an extremely low-oxygen environment at extreme temperatures to produce flammable gases that can then be used to generate heat and electricity. It produces biochar as a byproduct that helps trap CO_2. The biochar can be worked into the soil to increase yields and lock up excess CO_2 for many years. Because of this, it is suggested that it may help in the fight against global warming.

Those are some of the techniques that can be used to create a more "permaculture" greenhouse. The key is to use your imagination, learn new techniques, and use the materials you have on hand. What follows are some ideas for the actual construction of a greenhouse.

Greenhouses Built from Recycled Materials

Minigreenhouses from plastic bottles

Several possibilities exist for using recycled materials for your greenhouse. There are greenhouses out there that have been constructed mostly from plastic bottles. That takes the plastic out of the environment and puts it to good, positive use. Similarly, old pipes and recycled windows can be used. The pipes can be used to make the frame and the windows form the transparent walls and ceiling. This is an excellent permaculture project if you are replacing the windows in your main building to improve energy efficiency. There are many greenhouses out there that are made entirely from recycled windows.

Greenhouses Built from Converted Structures

You can easily convert an old shed or barn if you remove the opaque walls, leaving the frame in place, and then replace the walls with glass or plastic. Another possibility is a breezeway or a garage that is no longer needed. Again, remove the ceiling and walls and replace them with a transparent medium.

Greenhouses Built with Standard Materials

Of course, there is nothing wrong with going the traditional route and building a greenhouse from standard materials. You need a frame and, as the other examples show, siding made of glastic, plastic, or some similar material. The soap bubble greenhouse mentioned above, although advanced, would fall in this category, as would many other greenhouses built with more common forms of glazing.

Building a greenhouse need not be a complicated affair, and it makes a wonderful, effective addition to a permaculture garden.

Chapter 8: Incorporating Solar Power

Almost all life on Earth depends on the sun as its original source of light and heat. The sun warms the oceans and the land, causing the shifting of air currents and the changing of the weather. The sun, in conjunction with the tilt of the Earth, determines the changing seasons and the different climates that cover the globe.

What Is Solar Energy?

The sun provides two main forms of energy: light and heat. Both types are useful from a permaculture perspective. Light allows us to see and navigate through our gardens—that's an obvious benefit. A more subtle benefit is that plants use sunlight in photosynthesis to change carbon dioxide into oxygen and several other useful byproducts.

Without the light from the sun, not only would we not be able to see, but we also wouldn't be able to breathe. This is one of the reasons why climate activists are concerned about environmental challenges like deforestation. Without plants to change carbon dioxide (CO_2) into oxygen, the CO_2 levels in the atmosphere will rise, and oxygen levels will decrease. CO_2 is believed to cause the greenhouse effect, and oxygen is needed to support life.

The heat from the sun is another important element that assists the development of life. Without heat, plants would never blossom and produce fruit, nor would most kinds of animals be able to survive. Likewise, we need heat to keep our bodies warm, blood flowing, and our organs working.

Basically, without either one of these elements, we die.

In the last several decades, solar power has evolved and become more efficient. Solar power refers to the harnessing of sunlight to produce electricity. Sunlight is used to stimulate the motion of electrons, which in turn generates electricity. This process, called the photovoltaic effect, is driving the technology behind solar power.

To incorporate solar power and use it in your permaculture endeavor, you need a solar power system.

How Does A Solar Power System Work?

A solar power system is dependent upon several pieces of technology. These include solar panels, an inverter, racking, and, possibly, batteries and charge controllers.

• Solar panels are one of the key components of a solar power system. They are the doorway through which solar energy enters our control. Sunlight strikes the panels and, through the photovoltaic effect, is converted into electricity.

• An inverter is another key component of a solar power system. There are two forms of electricity: direct current (DC) and alternating current (AC). Most modern-day appliances run on alternating currents. This is because the electricity you get from your outlets at home is alternating current. Although there are some uses for direct current, the larger market by far is alternating current. Solar panels produce direct current. An inverter is a technology that takes that direct current and transforms it (inverts it) into alternating current.

• Racking is the term used to refer to the physical supports of your solar power system. The racking holds the panels in place.

• Batteries can form part of a solar power system when used to store the power generated from the system to be used later.

• Charge Controllers control the rate at which said batteries are allowed to charge when attached to the system.

Those are the main components of a solar power system. There are a few other smaller elements (fuses, wiring, etc.), but there is no need to get granular here.

Benefits of Renewable Energy

There are many distinct benefits to renewable energy in general and solar energy in particular. Using renewable energy is also a central focus in permaculture and reduces needless waste while utilizing energy found in your permaculture garden (including sunlight). The following is a list of benefits of solar energy:

Solar Energy is Renewable: The sun is a star. Its expected life runs in the billions of years. That makes it an almost infinite resource. So we can harvest its rays over and over again.

Solar Energy Can Lower Your Electric Bills: Solar energy can be used to either augment the energy you get from a power plant or even replace it entirely. Either way, it will lower electric bills. Properly set up and run, it may be able to reduce utility bills to $0 or even provide a nominal return on your monthly bill.

Solar Energy Can Provide Remote Power: If you live on a mountainside or other remote area, solar power might be your best or only option for power, particularly if it proves impossible to supply power lines to your home.

Solar Energy Increases Your Property Value: Homes with their own solar power systems sell for a higher price than homes without. As "green energy" becomes more and more effective and desirable, this added bonus will likely become even more pronounced.

Solar Energy Allows You to Take Your Electronics "Off the Grid": Solar technology has improved over the years. Many solar power systems have evolved to the point where they are as easy to use as just plugging a cord into an outlet. Many systems are also portable and expandable. This allows you to take almost anything you want "off the grid." You can charge your iPhone, tablet, or electric mower with solar energy.

Solar Power Can Make Your Living/Workspace More Comfortable: Solar power can be used to heat and cool your home through the use of solar air heaters—some of which are built from recycled materials. There are also solar air conditioners that run on solar power and run more efficiently than most traditional cooling options.

Solar Power Is Becoming More Affordable: One of the miracles of capitalism is that most technological products usually become drastically less and less expensive the more time passes. The same is true with solar power. Costs continue to drop, and their uses continue to expand. It is really becoming an integral part of our world.

Why Is Solar Power Better than Standard Electricity?

In the short term, you may save some money because solar power is often offered at a discounted rate. Similarly, as the green movement influences more political systems globally, things like carbon taxes and renewable subsidies become more prevalent. Solar power will help you to avoid carbon taxes and perhaps take advantage of the subsidies. In many cases, you can choose to purchase your system from the financing company, become completely electricity-independent, and reduce your energy bills to virtually zero. It might take some investment initially, but the longer you run a solar system, the more money you will save.

What Can Be Powered by Solar Energy?

Anything that runs on electricity can potentially be powered by solar energy. Perhaps the better, more pertinent question, is "What kinds of things are powered by solar energy today?" So far, solar power has expanded into the market in many areas. Small electronics like outdoor solar lights and solar-powered calculators run on their own integrated solar panels, and larger items like golf carts, RVs, and boats are powered by solar panels or use batteries charged by solar panels. In some places, entire homes and businesses are run solely on solar power, and there are even residences that have excess solar power that is fed back into the grid, bringing an income to the owners of the house. Solar power is an ideal power source for permaculture and homesteading.

Solar Water Heating and Other Larger Homesteading Ideas

There are several applications of solar power on a permaculture homestead. This list is always expanding, but even at present, it is already fairly wide-ranging. Some large homestead systems that can be handled by solar power include:

Solar Electricity: A solar PV (photovoltaic) system can be installed on the roof of any home or building to help offset the cost of electricity. In some cases, solar power might be able to provide for a building's entire electrical needs. Excess solar power from such a system can be stored in batteries and then used to supply needs when more energy is required than is being produced.

Solar Water Heating: One significant use of solar energy on a permaculture homestead is to heat water. Although in most cases, solar energy is used to heat the water that is used inside a home, there is no reason why the same system cannot help heat water in a greenhouse or anywhere else on a homestead.

Solar Space Heating: Another possibility is to use solar power for space heating. These systems sometimes include radiant floors or Forced Hot Air systems. Passive solar home design can also serve this purpose by making use of careful placement of windows and selection of building materials for the home.

Solar Ventilation: Solar attic fans have an obvious application for use in a home's attic. However, as greenhouses may also sometimes need ventilation, solar attic fans can likely serve that function. A permaculture homestead can use such a system in both places.

Solar Lighting: Solar lights are virtually ubiquitous. They can be in gardens, on road signs, streetlights, and anywhere around the home and garden. A permaculture homestead could use them to light their gardens during the night, if required, or provide light to any other location that sees a lot of nighttime use.

Portable Solar: As noted above, solar power has several portable systems. The world is filled with phones, tablets, and other electrical items that constantly need to be charged. A portable solar PV charger can serve that need effectively. The near future may see PV technology being incorporated into our phones on a large scale (the technology for such phones already exists). Other advances are constantly in the works.

Solar Transportation: RVs, boats, and golf carts were mentioned above as options for solar power systems. Of these three forms of transportation, the one that seems most applicable to a permaculture homestead would be the golf cart. Imagine you have several acres on your homestead. Do you want to walk across it to get to your Zone 4 or Zone 5? Or would you rather drive down a dirt trail instead? Obviously, you would not want to use something powered by fossil fuels, so a solar-powered golf cart or something similar would be ideal.

Renewable energy is becoming more prevalent, and the technology that utilizes it is constantly improving, being refined, and becoming more efficient. Even if there wasn't an environmental issue to worry about, renewable energy is here to stay. Renewable energy helps to improve our lives and battle environmental challenges to produce a cleaner world in which to live.

Solar Panels in a Home

If you are considering a permaculture space, you might be interested in more information about solar power and solar panels.

Solar panels are the technology that captures the light from the sun and transforms it into electricity. A solar panel consists of a grid of solar cells. Each solar cell is made largely from silicon, an element on the periodic table chosen for its conductive properties. Silicon generates an electric current when it is exposed to light and undergoes the photovoltaic effect. The solar cell harnesses that current.

A solar cell is typically a 6" x 6" square of silicon with electrical plates attached to its face. There is a protective sheet of material on the back of the solar panel, and on the front, a sheet of glass. The light passes through glass, activates the silicon, and you get electricity.

Solar cells that are tied into the same single output are called a panel. Solar panels that are grouped together in a system are called an array.

If you decide to incorporate a solar panel system on your permaculture homestead, one of the first decisions you'll have to make is whether you want the energy to go back into the electrical grid (a grid-tie system) or if you want it stored in a collection of batteries. Of course, if you are not connected to the electrical grid to begin with, this decision is made for you.

Given the option, you might want to give the excess power back to the electrical grid and look at it as an implementation of Tenet #3 (returning surplus to public use). If you do so, you are compensated for it with credits given to you by the utility company.

One thing you need to be aware of, though, is the net metering policy of your utility. This outlines how the company bills you. Often, the utility will buy the electricity from you at the same rate that it sells it to you. Sometimes, though, it does not, and that can seriously affect your return on investment when going solar.

According to unboundsolar.com, "Most manufacturers guarantee under warranty that their panels will be at least 80% efficient for 25 years." This does not mean that the panels will suddenly deteriorate and drop to 0% in their twenty-sixth year. No, they should last several years longer, but produce less electricity in that timeframe. But, of course, you still must take that drop-off in output into account when determining whether or not you wish to incorporate solar power into your permaculture homestead.

If you get a 300-watt system that will deteriorate to 240 watts at year 25, you shouldn't design a system to run on more than 240 watts unless you plan on compensating for it when the output wattage begins to drop off.

Another consideration is the fact that other elements like batteries and inverters have shorter lifespans than the panels. Therefore, you may replace them once or twice over that the lifespan of your solar panels, which is another cost you must factor in.

Effects of Solar Panels on Energy Use

It is worth pointing out that, although going solar will not affect the total amount of energy you use, it will make the energy you use cleaner. And, going solar will likely give you lower electric bills or may even eliminate them entirely. And that is something worth doing.

Chapter 9: Learning to Compost

Many gardeners and farmers use compost. Permaculture gardeners are no exception. Composting plays a critical role in the permaculture journey. Overall, it is a natural fit for the permaculture lifestyle because its use incorporates and embodies many permaculture principles.

What Is Composting?

Composting is a process used to create your own natural fertilizer and soil amendment. It uses natural materials in conjunction with organic material to achieve this. For example, you might have leftover potato peels, celery leaves, or eggshells that you won't be eating. If you combine these with shredded newspaper, cardboard, and leaves, such waste can be added to a compost pile.

A compost pile consists of organic waste that breaks down into a nutrient-rich soil amendment over a period of time lasting from few months to a year or more, depending upon how the pile is treated. It is a relatively simple practice that can reap huge rewards for your garden.

Composting Works by Balancing Four Different Elements in the Compost Pile:

1. Carbon: Carbon-rich materials include organic matter like hay, dry leaves, and shredded paper. When mixed into the compost, they provide food and energy for microorganisms, allowing them to break down the materials in the compost pile.

2. Nitrogen: Nitrogen-rich materials include organic matter like fresh grass clippings, fruit and vegetable scraps from the kitchen, and coffee grounds. These provide the protein for the microorganisms to multiply and grow.

3. Water: The right amount of water helps break down the compost pile by helping dissolve the matter while nourishing the microorganism as they do their work. Take note, however; too much water may drown your microorganisms, while not enough will lead to dehydration.

4. Oxygen: Microorganisms need oxygen to work efficiently. The compost pile needs to be aerated regularly by turning it regularly with either a pitchfork or a tumbling bin. Failure to do so may cause sluggish activity by the microorganisms.

When all these elements are in balance and work effectively together, the microorganisms in your compost pile will transform it into a pile of rich organic matter that can be a soil amendment or fertilizer.

Benefits of Composting

Compost can be a soil amendment or fertilizer for your permaculture garden. It provides many benefits, including:

Repurposing and Recycling Organic Matter: This incorporates permaculture Principle #2: Catch and Store Energy. Organic matter is an excellent source of energy for your garden, and it comes in many forms. It is also good for the environment because it instills the habit of recycling and reusing in your daily activities.

Eliminating Waste: This is another permaculture principle (#6: Produce No Waste). Again, it is good for the environment and the planet. It will also help clean out your refrigerator in an eco-friendly way.

Improving Soil Structure: Whatever soil you start with, be it hard and compacted, heavy, stony, wet, or sandy, it will benefit from adding compost. According to www.gardeners.com, "Adding compost will improve [your soil's] texture, water-holding capacity, and fertility."

Providing Plant Nutrients: No matter how healthy your soil is at the start of your journey, it will eventually exhaust itself unless its nutrient content is continually replenished. Compost serves that end. It nutrifies the plants in the soil as and when needed, lengthening the soil's productive life.

Stimulating Beneficial Organisms: Compost is rich in both nutrients and microorganisms that benefit your plants and flowers. The microorganisms help convert nutrients into a form more readily usable by your plants and generally improve the soil and attract other macro-level organisms like earthworms, millipedes, and other creatures. These macro-organisms burrow through your soil, creating spaces that allow air and water to reach the roots of your plants, and when they die, they compost back into the earth too.

Providing Chemical Moderation for Your Garden: Due to its constituent chemicals and nutrients, compost can help moderate your garden's pH levels in a healthy, natural fashion, so you needn't waste time measuring the pH content nor adding chemicals to regulate it. The plants in your garden can access the nutrients in your compost as they need it, in amounts as large or as small as they need.

Building Healthy Soil: Whether you apply it in the spring or the fall, compost improves the health of your soil. In the spring, it will help nutrify your plants as the growing season begins; in the fall, it will nourish the organisms still active in the warm soil despite dropping temperatures in the air.

There are many benefits to using compost. Compost helps nourish not only your plants but the many beneficial organisms—both microscopic and macroscopic—your plants and soil need to remain healthy.

How Do You Begin Composting?

Now that you understand what composting is and some benefits that come from composting, you may be interested in starting your own compost pile for your permaculture site.

What to Start With:

A compost pile generally begins as a mixture of various organic materials placed together to decompose into a nutrient-rich mound of organic matter that can amend and fertilize the soil. You can use many organic materials to build your compost. These include:

- Alfalfa Meal (green)

- Coffee Grounds (green)

- Corncobs and Stalks (brown)

- Dry Leaves (brown)

- Eggshells (although these are very durable and take a longer time to break down; they can also be sprinkled on gardens to deter slugs) (green)

- Feathers or Hair (green)

- Fresh Leaves (green)

- Fresh Weeds (green)

- Fruit Scraps (green)

- Grass Clippings (green)

- Kitchen Scraps (green)

- Pine Needles (brown)

- Rotted Manure (green)

- Sawdust (untreated wood only) (brown)

- Seaweed (green)

- Shredded Newspaper (brown)

- Straw (brown)

- Vegetable Scraps (green)

- Vegetable Stalks (brown)

- Wood Scraps (finely chopped) and/or bark chips (brown)

Each item in the above list is denoted green or brown. Green refers to nitrogen-rich materials, and brown refers to carbon-rich materials. If you have too many brown materials, it will take a long time (maybe even years) for your pile to decompose because there is too little protein for your microbes. But if you have too many green materials, it will take a long time to decompose, and the pile will likely get soggy and smelly because there isn't enough material to feed your microbes. We will discuss both of those a little bit more below.

What Materials Should You Avoid Using?

The following is a list of materials you should avoid using as they can cause gardening problems, make the compost pile smell, and attract unwanted pests and animals.

- Cat/Dog feces

- Dairy Products

- Diseased plant materials.

- Meat grease, fat, and oil.

- Pressure-treated wood.

- Weeds with seeds.

Note: many people also believe that onions, garlic, and citrus peels should not be included in your compost pile because they repel earthworms, and earthworms can be a critical part of your garden. There is also a line of thinking that everything can be composted if done properly. We recommend starting with green and brown materials and researching the layering processes needed to break down the organic material not normally composted.

What Tools Do You Need?

The only tools you need to start a compost pile are the respective organic materials outlined above, plus a container to store them in, a pitchfork to turn the pile periodically, and a hose or other method to deliver water to the materials. However, some people don't like the hassle of turning the pile to keep it aerated. In such cases, these measures can also be taken:

- Build your pile on a pile of branches or a raised platform made of wood to allow the air to circulate.

- Put a couple of perforated plastic pipes (4") through the middle of the pile.

- You can also invest in bins that can be turned by hand, flipping the entire container to mix the organic matter.

What Type of Bins Should You Use?

Compost bins have been mentioned several times. The following are some standard options for compost bins:

- **Stationary Plastic Bins:** These bins should measure around 3 feet by 3 feet by 3 feet. Many units possess air vents on the side to aid in the aeration process. Often, they are designed for continuous composting as opposed to batch composting. As an added plus, they can be made of recycled plastics. If there are no vents, you can always drill your own holes to allow aeration and drainage.

• **Rotating or Tumbling Bins:** These bins are designed for making batches of compost. First, you collect the material and shred it. Then, you place the material in the bin and rotate it daily. Provided you have a well-balanced compost pile (in terms of green and brown materials), you should be able to produce a pile of excellent compost after several weeks.

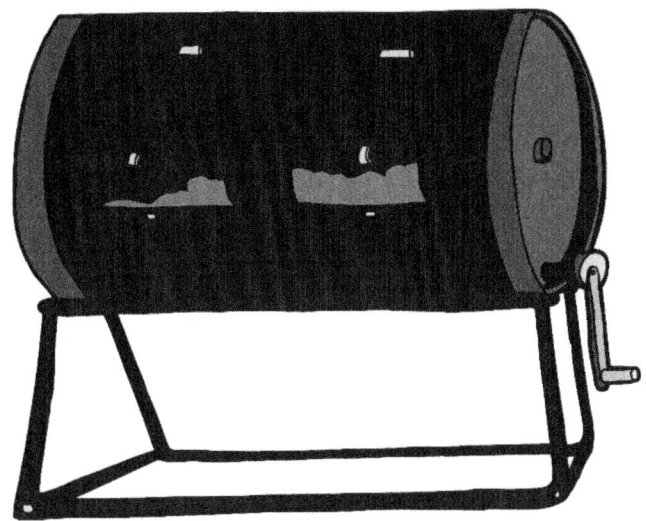

• **Worm Composter:** Vermicomposting is a type of composting that uses worms to speed up the process. Worms are very effective at decomposing organic matter. They are particularly good when it comes to kitchen scraps. However, be warned that worms generally cannot tolerate high temperatures. To use vermicomposting, you need a watertight container of some sort to put the scraps and worms in, and then you must store them somewhere that allows you to keep the temperature between 50 degrees F and 80 degrees F at all times.

Any of these composting bins are available commercially. Alternatively, you can make your own from many common materials. For example, one excellent method involves making a wire bin from fencing wire you can get from your local hardware store (or have lying around). Another method uses a partially-buried perforated trash can. Another involves using bricks or stones (spaced for aeration purposes) to build the walls of the composter. Or use wood pallets: one to form the base, four to form the walls, and a tarp to cover the whole thing. With a little bit of research online, you should have no difficulty building your own composting bin.

Types of Composting and How They Differ

Composting is a remarkably easy method to recycle many kinds of natural waste produced by your permaculture site. There are three basic kinds of composting: aerobic composting (also called hot composting), anaerobic composting (also called cold composting) and vermicomposting (composting with worms).

Aerobic Composting (Hot Composting)

Aerobic composting is composting that involves the use of free-flowing oxygen. As a rule, it requires more effort than the other kinds of composting, but it usually produces results in a shorter period of time, particularly compared to anaerobic composting. Aerobic composting in warm weather usually produces compost within one to three months. This process carefully manages the four composting ingredients–nitrogen, carbon, air, and water–to feed and grow a proper population of microorganisms that speed up decay. The key is to add sufficient quantities of green compost materials (see above), which the microorganisms feed on. As they feed on them, they produce large amounts of heat and warm up the compost pile. This gives aerobic composting its alternate name of "hot composting." There are four basic steps to aerobic composting.

- **Step 1: Combine Both Brown and Green Matter Together:** It's a good idea to wait until you have enough material to fill a cubic yard before you begin. Once you have your material, you should combine your "brown" items (dry and carbon-rich) with your "green" items (wet and nitrogen-rich). It is usually recommended that you mix three parts of brown material with one part green. If the pile starts to look soggy and smell, you can add more brown material. If it gets too dry and brown, you can add more green material.

- **Step 2: Water the Pile**: You can add water to the pile with a hose or watering can but be careful not to add too much. If you drown the microorganisms, the pile will rot and not compost. You should also monitor the temperature using a thermometer or by shoving your hand into the center of the pile (nothing like getting right in there). It should feel warm.

- **Step 3: Stir the Pile**: As this is an aerobic process, the pile needs oxygen. This is obtained by periodically stirring the pile with a pitchfork or a tumbling bin. The optimum temperature for turning is between 130- and 150-degrees F, or when the center feels warm.

- **Step 4: Feed the Garden**: When the compost stops giving off heat and has transformed into a pile of dry, brown, crumbly matter, it is ready for use. Add several inches as needed to your flower beds, vegetable gardens, and lawns.

If you are not in a rush, turning the pile frequently is not required. Hot compost piles are usually turned every three to five days, depending on the interior temperature (if it drops below 110 degrees F, it's time to turn). If you don't wish to turn the pile at all, you are better off using the anaerobic composting process.

Anaerobic Composting (Cold Composting)

Anaerobic composting is relatively simple compared to hot composting. All you need to do is to collect the yard waste and kitchen scraps you would use in hot composting, place them all together in a pile or bin, and wait. The composting will take care of itself, but it may take a year or longer. In addition to the length of time, cold composting is also frequently accompanied by powerful odors. This is a result of certain bacteria that appears when there is little to no oxygen available. A similar thing happens in landfills.

Vermicomposting (Using Worms)

As stated above, vermicomposting involves the use of worms in conjunction with oxygen and moisture. Worms are added to your pile or box of organic matter, at which point they begin to eat the matter and release nitrogen-rich castings. Not every type of worm will be usable here. Most people recommend redworms, which are also known as "red wigglers." The worms do most of the work in this process. It has the advantage of little odor and fewer dangerous bacteria or methane. The process can be done indoors if needed, there is no need to turn, the compost is easily harvested, and it takes only a few minutes of effort per week. As an added bonus, the worms become part of the household, and many kids like to take care of them. Worms used in composting enjoy the following types of organic matter:

- Grains like bread, pasta, rice, and oatmeal.

- Non-acidic vegetable and fruit scraps.

- Aged (a few days) manure from herbivores like cows, rabbits, horses, etc.

- Crushed clean eggshells for grit.

- Grass clippings and fallen leaves.

They do not enjoy:

- Meats, oily foods, and dairy products.

Many people highly recommend vermicomposting, provided you don't mind the worms.

The use of compost is a critical part of a permaculture garden, whether it be produced aerobically, anaerobically, or with the help of worms. Each type of composting has its own pros and cons, and opinions vary on which is the best. You'll have to make up your own mind about which is best for you based on the time you have and the type of permaculture garden. What is clear is that compost has many benefits. Like many other permaculture techniques, it serves multiple functions, from recycling materials to amending the soil. It has a variety of benefits that are not easily matched. If you plan to garden, you should plan to compost.

Chapter 10: Managing the Water Supply

There are many different aspects to a permaculture system. By this point, you should have a basic grasp of everything from gardening to the proper use of space to the making of compost. As mentioned in many previous sections, one of the critical elements of permaculture is a focus on reusing, renewing, and recycling, as well as focusing on incorporating nature and its resources into your lifestyle. Because of that, there is an emphasis in permaculture on using natural sources of water, such as rainfall, instead of that which can be obtained from a city supply. Acquiring, using, and manipulating water and its flows merits a discussion in its own right. This brings the discussion to the next critical component of permaculture: water management.

What Is Water Management?

Water management consists of the harvesting and manipulating natural water and natural water-flows for use by your permaculture system. Whether you want to collect water in ponds, build dams, or simply sink runoff into the soil, you will need to know about and incorporate various water management skills.

In this regard, the goal of permaculture design is to harvest and retain as much naturally flowing water on your site as you possibly can. This includes rainfall and other natural sources you might have on-site (rivers, creeks, springs, etc.). Whatever water you capture must be stored in the soil or stored on the surface in ponds, tanks, or other containers.

The approach to achieve good water management involves slowing, spreading, and sinking water that appears on your permaculture site. You want to maximize the use of this water by collecting as much as you can, storing excess water for dry periods, and distributing that which is needed across your site.

The amount of water you can capture and store depends on various factors, including the condition of your soil, the terrain in which you live, your climate, your budget, and more.

As you begin your water management strategy, the first thing you'll need to do is to assess your site in terms of its needs and available resources. Ask yourself, "How do I intend to use this water?" Do you need it for your home, fish production, irrigation, or to provide for your livestock on-site?

Once you have a general idea of how you will use your water, you need to identify your water sources. You'll also have to assess the frequency and infrequency of rainfall and maybe even do a few calculations to determine your site's rainfall volume (area of watershed x average annual rainfall). Your planning will have to adjust accordingly. If you get most of your rainwater from just a few high-intensity rainfalls, it will impact your water strategies very differently than if you get the bulk of your rain spread out relatively evenly throughout the year.

Also of great significance is the area of your watershed and your place within it. If you are at a higher elevation in the hills or mountains, you'll likely get far less water flowing through your area than you would if you lived in the lowlands. The trade-off is, of course, that the water will be fresher. As rainwater runs down mountainsides and hills, it may collect undesirable chemicals, sediments, etc., from other sites (i.e., if it passes through land where artificial fertilizers are being used).

Once you identify your water sources and needs, you have to start making plans on how you will store water that comes onto your site. There are basically two places to store water: in the ground or on the surface.

Your first priority should be to store as much water in the soil as possible because that is the cheapest place to store it and most likely the largest storage resource you have on your site. You might have other long-term plans for a vast interconnected network of irrigation channels but start with the simplest and cheapest place: the soil. Your first objective to deal with rainfall is to slow, spread, and sink the water. The next objective is to build up and grow the organic matter in the soil. The first of these objectives will, to a certain extent, help the second objective. Irrigated soil is more likely to develop healthier organic matter than dry soil. Life needs water to survive and grow. Wet soil provides that; dry soil does not.

The easiest way to do this is to let the rain fall directly on your crops. You can lock in this moisture by adding some ground cover to the top of the soil. If an area is covered by heavy growth or trees, you can add irrigation channels to divert falling rain where you want it to go.

Once you've appropriately planned for your water storage, you need to develop a plan for water harvesting. This may involve such things as a rain barrel system to collect runoff from the roof of your house or other methods to collect runoff from other impervious structures or even over land. This can mean building swales, ponds, dams, or even redirecting flows from creeks that cross your land. You have a lot of options that you'll need to explore.

The first and most obvious of these storage options is a rain barrel water system.

Rain Barrel Water System

The first point to be made when discussing a rain barrel water system is a legal one. Depending on where you live, certain ordinances or laws may regulate the collection of rainwater. So, the first thing you'll need to do is check with your local authorities regarding such laws and regulations.

The next point concerns possible contaminants in the water you collect. Before using and especially before drinking your collected water, make sure you test it and set up a purification process to deal with contaminants.

The simplest form of a rain barrel water system involves collecting rainwater from the roof of your house. Most houses have an eavestrough system that redirects runoff to a few downspouts to shuttle the water away from the base of the house and relieve potential erosion problems. Such downspouts can be used to collect rainwater by placing a collection barrel at the bottom of the spout.

These barrels will have the following necessary features. There will be a faucet/nozzle near the bottom to access the collected water for use. The barrel will need an overflow hole/hose near the top to deal with excess water when the barrel is filled (this can flow into another barrel or away from your house). The top should provide some mechanism to filter the water (a thin metal mosquito screen, perhaps) when it enters the barrel. You might be able to purchase such a barrel pre-made, but if not, you should have little difficulty constructing your own from another type of barrel or container, be it new plastic garbage can or a wooden barrel. Supplies can likely be purchased at your local hardware and plumbing stores.

Rainwater is an excellent resource for the gardens and animals on your property. Not only is it a free resource, but it has more nutrients than tap water and saves you money.

Why Is Water Management a Beneficial Part of Permaculture?

Water management is critical to permaculture largely because it provides several key benefits to the site on which it is used and even to the larger community as a whole.

Over the last few decades, many people have noticed what they believe to be strange and detrimental developments in the weather. Under the assumption that this weird weather will continue and worsen, the need to develop extreme weatherproof systems is readily apparent. These systems must be resilient and adaptive, allowing us to manage where there is too much water and where there is not enough.

Water management techniques that allow us to combine earthworks, irrigation systems, and soil-building may allow us to cope with such difficulties and perhaps even reverse some of their effects.

Using permaculture-based water management concepts and techniques isn't just about maximizing the use of the water we have. It is also about fighting and reducing erosion that unmanaged water might produce, bringing life back to even the most arid of lands, fighting climate change and its effects, improving agricultural production, and building and improving topsoil.

Permaculture Water Management Techniques for Your Land

Permaculture-based water management techniques provide you with various tools and methods to dig into your land to better hold and distribute the water that enters your site.

Ponds and Tanks

Ponds and tanks provide two important ways of storing water on the surface of your land. If you can manage it, setting up a water tank at a high point on your land, like at the top of a hill, will allow you to use gravity to access and use the water instead of a pump or other mechanical assistance.

A pond might be better suited for a lower-level point on your land because gravity will serve to feed it naturally. Ponds, in particular, are an excellent resource to have as they can be used for many different purposes. For example, they can be used as a wildlife habitat for aquaculture, irrigation, recreation, or simply for domestic water storage.

There are two basic types of ponds: an embankment pond and an excavation pond. An embankment pond is built by damming up a stream, creek, or another watercourse where the corresponding valley is sufficiently depressed to allow you to store enough water for your needs. On the other hand, an excavated pond requires you to dig out the whole storage area on level, or mostly level, ground. Excavated ponds involve a smaller amount of water than an embankment pond. In some instances, you might use a combination of excavation and embankment.

Swales

Swales are another technique used to slow, spread, and sink water. They are designed to capture and hold runoff water from storms or floods. Once captured in the swale, the water is allowed to seep into the soil to be stored.

A swale is a shallow trench dug across the contours of a piece of land to whatever length is required. The earth removed from the swale is used to build a berm (a raised mound of earth) on the downhill side. As a result, runoff water flowing down the hill will be stopped by the berm and collected in the trench of the swale. Excess water will flow over the berm and continue downhill, but the soil will slowly absorb the rest for use.

This changes the flow pattern of the runoff from an overland flow to a more useful underground one. The water captured can be accessed to irrigate your land, and even if it is left to sit and sink into the soil, you will find that vegetation will grow quite readily and happily on the downside of the berm. In addition, it will help improve the soil quality of the earth in and around the swale.

Another side benefit of swales is that they help prevent gullies by decreasing the erosive power of rainwater runoff.

Keyline Design

According to the World Permaculture Association, "Key Line Design uses the form and shape of the land to determine the layout and position of farm dams, irrigation areas, roads, fences, farm buildings, and tree lines." A critical component of Keyline Design is keyline agriculture, whose most fundamental technique involves spreading water from the wet areas of your land to the dry areas. This is achieved by using a tractor to dig furrows in the ground with a keyline plow that runs perpendicular to the land's slope.

The idea is to change the natural flow of runoff water. Normally, water will flow downhill from high points to low points. However, with the keyline design, the flowing water is intercepted by the keyline furrow. Thus, the water is diverted to a perpendicular path parallel to the keyline instead of downslope.

The ultimate effect of this is that the furrows hold significant quantities of water, allowing the water to sink into the soil instead of flowing downslope to be lost. Much like the case of the swale, more water permeates the soil allowing for greater plant growth and an increase in soil microbes.

The Vallerani System

The Vallerani System is a method developed using a specialized tractor-like vehicle called a Delfino. The method consists of working semi-arid to arid land in such a way as to bring back life to it and rejuvenate the soil that has been degraded. With the Delfino, you can dig hundreds of micro-basins which are almost like miniature swales that will collect and slow natural water flows. The water collected will sink into the soil and, over time, rejuvenate the land.

Imprinting

Another method involving a different specialized tractor-like machine is called imprinting. It was developed by Dr. Robert Dixon, who has been successfully experimenting with it since 1976.

The land imprinting vehicle rolls a "plow" shaped like an 8-pointed star across the desert, leaving hundreds or even thousands of tiny pits in the ground. When the wind blows, the pits collect various things like seeds, rabbit droppings, and other small quantities of biological matter. Then, when the rain comes, the pits collect a small amount of rain to work with that matter. The water spreads into a localized area around the pit and creates positive conditions for life to grow.

Trincheras and Gabions

Another method used to harness water flows and restore land involves the use of trincheras and gabions. A trinchera is a small dam of gathered rocks used to check the flow of runoff and other waters. They are used to harvest rainwater and restore drylands. The gabion method uses trincheras on a large scale. Much like the previously discussed methods, the general idea is to slow down the water flow to give it a chance to sink into the soil, where it will rejuvenate the land. It is particularly useful when most of your annual rainfall falls in a few intense storms instead of being spread out over the year. Again, like many of the other methods, this method also reduces erosion.

Water Retention Landscapes

A water retention landscape is more of a general term to describe multiple methods across a single region of land. For example, you might use a combination of swales, man-made lakes, and terraces to rejuvenate a region. These landscapes help fight desertification and erosion, and even help reverse the effects of climate change.

As seen, you have several options available to help manage water on your permaculture site. Most of the techniques work in the same way. They slow water and allow it to sink into the soil. This creates a better environment in which life can grow. Similarly, erosion is reduced, and before you know it, what was once dry and desolate is now brimming with life.

You can transform almost any piece of land, but only with proper water management, making water management one of the most important aspects of permaculture.

Chapter 11: Reducing Household Waste

One truism of life is that almost every household produces waste. Some more than others, but the scope of the phenomenon is still nearly universal. Permaculture, as a discipline and a philosophical approach to living, tries to address that. Reducing waste and living more conservatively is a benchmark of the green movement in general and permaculture in particular.

But how do you go about doing so? Is it possible to eliminate waste entirely? If so, how?

The Need to Reduce Personal Waste

The first task in answering those questions is setting the stage and demonstrating the need to reduce personal waste in your everyday living. If you are well-ensconced in the green movement, you are probably well informed about the need. Still, it doesn't hurt to review the more salient reasons.

Reducing your personal waste reduces your environmental footprint, which is to say it reduces the stress you put on the environment in the course of your daily life. There are also economic advantages. The less waste you produce, the less waste you have to pay to have removed or otherwise disposed of. Similarly, recycling leads to the creation of recycling centers, leading to jobs for workers in the community. Then, there is the reduction in energy consumption— another bonus.

But don't get the impression that this is a simple task with a quick and easy solution. There is a marked need for waste reduction in everyday living. Some items cannot be recycled or can only be recycled with difficulty. Other times, the recycling infrastructure can't keep up with the enormous quantity of waste modern society produces or, perhaps, simply has no easy way to handle certain materials that find their way into the recycle bin.

In the United States, the EPA has tried to address this with their "Reduce, Reuse, Recycle" campaign. In theory, it is a good idea, and it has led to great progress. As time goes on and awareness is raised, more and more people are adopting those practices. Reusable shopping bags are becoming more common, as more cities are adopting plastic bag bans. More people are incorporating waste recycling into their daily living.

But is it enough?

Landfill Stats

Most waste produced in the modern household finds its way to a landfill. Of that waste, about one-third of it comes from packaging materials. Is that a problem in need of a solution? Can that stat be reduced? It's already well-established that cardboard works well in compost. How much could landfill waste be reduced if all the cardboard packaging material were put to such a use? Surely, that would have a dramatic impact.

Can we apply similar thinking to other landfill facts?

How about all the organic garbage (a full 1,200 pounds of it) that every American throws out each year? Surely, composting is a better answer there.

Likewise, reusing recyclable materials can go a long way in dealing with our glut of trash. For example, the U.S. population discards enough aluminum every year to rebuild the entire fleet of every commercial U.S. airline four times over. That's a lot of metal. At the same time, the population of the U.S. discards 1.6 billion pens, 16 billion diapers, 220 thousand car tires, and 2 billion razor blades every year. Surely, all that could be used for something.

Consider this interesting little fact: 10% of the purchase price of the average item sold is spent on the packaging of that item. And that packaging is typically thrown away. 65% of the trash in most households comes from packaging.

The U.S. produces more trash than any other country on the planet. Although the country has only 5% of the world's population, it generates 40% of the world's garbage—or approximately 1,609 pounds per person every year.

In some parts of the country, the trash is piled so high it makes a veritable hill. For example, just look up "Mount Rumpke" in Hamilton County, Ohio (go on, Google it now). It is a pile of trash that looms a full 1,045 feet above sea level.

All that being said, the obvious thing to do is to recycle as much trash as you can. It's the cheapest alternative, costing only $30 per ton compared to $50 for a landfill and $75 for incineration (Hat tip to usi.edu for all the stats).

How to Reduce Your Waste

If you are convinced that waste is a problem and you want to do something about it, start with just reducing the amount produced. That old mantra, "Reduce, reuse, and recycle," lists reduce first for a reason—it's the most important and effective of the three. For example, you can begin by avoiding foods sold in excess packaging or invest in reusable containers such as water bottles. Then, once you've reduced as much as you can, you can move on to reusing and recycling.

Find out what you can recycle in your area and what rules apply. If you can, try to purchase recycled items. This helps support the recycling industry by incorporating recycled goods back into the economy. One aspect of the economy you can support with recycling is art. Many artists make art from trash and other found items. Why not purchase their work or even donate supplies? It's a win-win.

Other items that can be recycled include greywater, garden and kitchen greenery (composting these is an excellent idea), and even electronics. Take stock of all your little-used possessions. If something is rarely used and carries no sentimental value, why not get rid of it by donating it to someplace that can make use of it?

It's good to develop the appropriate mindset and look for recycling opportunities wherever you go. For example, look at the packaging for your groceries. Can it be recycled, or is it destined for a landfill? Let the answer to that question shape your purchase.

Finally, get organized and plan out your recycling efforts. Record the amount of waste you throw out. Get some numbers down and use those to plan out a more effective strategy. The goal is to keep as much of your stuff away from the landfill for as long as possible, preferably forever.

One of the keys to reducing waste is to use fewer disposable items—things like plastic bags or fast food "to go" packaging. You should try to rent items instead of buying them when you can. You can also try growing more of your own food—and don't forget to compost the scraps or use them to feed your animals.

You should also put in every effort to recycle your metal waste. It shouldn't be too difficult. Metal can easily be reshaped or reused in other goods, and most of them fetch a few coins per pound.

Plastic packaging is the main source of household waste. Raw beans and rice, for example, often come in plastic bags—and that's just more waste that you have to deal with. Plastic wrappers can be used as stuffing for cushions or even just to fill a plastic bottle to make it sturdier for some other use.

Glass is another substance that makes up a substantial amount of our waste. However, it has an obvious solution: just reuse it. Most of the time, a glass bottle needs only be washed out and rinsed, and it's ready for reuse.

Depending upon how enthusiastic you are about permaculture, you may look into more environmentally-friendly solutions for dealing with human waste. For example, toilets use a considerable amount of water over time, and the waste they capture generally isn't used for any beneficial purpose.

One alternative to the standard toilet is the "thunderbox," which is basically a dry toilet used to produce powerful compost. You use it like any other toilet, but instead of flushing it when you are done, you throw in a couple of handfuls of sawdust or straw. The sawdust and straw absorb the moisture, which, in turn, eliminates the odor.

The thunderbox is designed with chambers. So, when one is full, you switch to the other. And by the time the second one is full, the first has dried into useful fertilizer.

Can You Repurpose These Items?

Containers, Cans, and Glass Jars: All these items can be repurposed into several useful things. They can be used as desk organizers, bathroom containers, or even to hold bulk items in the pantry. Have a spare, clean coffee can? Fill it with rice, or dry beans, or cereal.

Plastic Bags: Plastic Bags are another item with a lot of possible uses. They can be cut up to be used to wrap sandwiches, used as small garbage can liners, used to collect pet waste, or just reused at the grocery store. You've got a lot of options.

Newspapers, Paper Bags, and Other Paper Products: It's easy for paper products to build up in your home. But it's almost just as easy to find good uses for such things. For example, newspaper and paper bags can be turned into compostable pots for garden seeds. Alternatively, they could be used as wrapping paper or to make envelopes.

Plastic Soda Bottles, Plastic Gallon Jugs, and Other Plastic Containers: Plastic bottles of any sort are ideal for storing homemade cleaners—just make sure you label them appropriately. But that's not the limit of their use. Soda bottles can be repurposed into bird feeders, and a plastic jug can be transformed into a dustpan or a plastic scoop. One often-overlooked resource is the everyday plastic takeout container from your local restaurant. Most of these are dishwasher safe and readily reusable.

Towels, Clothes, and Bedding: Fabrics like old towels and clothes can find many applications after they've outlived their primary use. At the very least, an old towel can be cut up into rags. An old pair of jeans could be transformed into shorts or simply cut up into pieces to patch other clothing. The possibilities are only limited by your imagination.

Seeds: You don't have to eat every last bit of vegetable you produce. You could let a few plants go to seed at the end of the season, collect the seeds, and use the seeds collected the following season. That will save you the trouble and money of purchasing new seeds.

Dryer Sheets and Lint Trap Lint: You can also make use of what is normally laundry waste. Dryer sheets can be used to dust, clean off soap scum, wipe up pet hair, or even polish chrome. As for the lint you might collect from your lint trap, you can use it to make some more compostable pots for seeds or stuff it in a toilet roll core to create an excellent fire-lighter for camping.

Bathroom and Personal Hygiene Items: A particularly useful tool is an old toothbrush. It can be used to scrub and clean those places that are really difficult to get to, like grout lines. Similarly, they could be used to clean electronics or other delicate items or cleaned and then used as eyebrow brushes or hair color applicators. Toothpaste tubes can be transformed into small funnels with little effort. Empty deodorant sticks can be refilled and reused.

That's a short list of common household items that can be repurposed. Once you make the decision to put in the effort, figuring out new uses for items can be great fun—almost a game. There are certainly many different possibilities.

Chapter 12: Adding in Animals

The last aspect of a permaculture endeavor is animals. Animals bring several benefits to a permaculture farm or homestead. If it is to survive and thrive, any ecosystem will likely incorporate a modest number of animals, big or small. The same is true of a permaculture ecosystem. The difference is that where permaculture is involved, knowledgeable human oversight is required.

Animals increase the biodiversity of any site to which they are added. This is a direct application of permaculture principles 8 (Integrate, Don't Separate) and 10 (Use and Value Diversity), and it has many powerful benefits.

Benefits of Having Animals on a Permaculture Property

On a permaculture homestead, much of your food and many other resources are provided by trees and other plants. However, when you add animals, you augment your food supplies—as you now have access to meat and, probably, eggs as well—and provide yourself with many resources like manure, skins, feathers and fur, and even a certain form of free labor.

For example, on many permaculture sites, the overgrowth of certain nuisance plants like grass, brambles, and weeds can be a problem. However, if you incorporate several grazing animals like goats or cows to feed on such plants, what was once a problem is now a steady supply of food for them. Additionally, as the animals eliminate the excess plants, they provide you with manure and food resources like meat and milk and possibly other yields like leather and fur.

The above example also demonstrates another benefit of adding animals to your permaculture site: the natural tendency of animals to do useful work. By feeding on the nuisance plants, your grazing animals clear the area for you. This saves fuel and man-hours that would have been required if the plants were cleared with trimmers or other machinery. Keep this in mind whenever you add an animal to your site, be it worms, chickens, or goats; they can do all sorts of useful work. It is up to you to identify that work potential and make use of it.

Another great example is to allow chickens to graze a grassy area to rid it of harmful insects, chop the grass nice and neat, and fertilize the soil with their poop.

Much like the plants discussed in other chapters, each animal fills its own ecological niche in the overall permaculture system and, as a result, serves as its own multi-functional component of that system.

Different animals perform different roles. For example, where chickens might scratch up the soil and feed on grubs, goats might feed on nuisance plants while providing milk. Cows, worms, and other animals will fill their own unique roles as well.

This makes the whole ecology of the permaculture system a single cohesive whole of interrelated parts.

Another, perhaps more subtle advantage to adding animals to your site is that the animals will draw your attention to different parts of your property. It is just a fact that animals require more attention than plants. So, as the animals move about or are rotated about your property, your focus will travel with them. As a result, you will regularly visit different parts of your property. This may have the benefit of helping you keep an eye on those parts which might have deteriorated from neglect. In other words, animals can serve as a discipline boost to help you maintain your property—particularly if you set up grazing patterns with that notion in mind.

The positive impact of animals on ecosystems is a firmly established fact. Animals improve fertility by working the soil and depositing manure. They increase biodiversity by improving the soil and its constitution, improve water retention in the soil by breaking impacted clods, provide weed control by eating unwanted plants and weeds, and provide control of pests—again, by eating the little critters.

Crucial to the proper use of animals is managing them in time and space through a practice called "Intense Rotational Grazing." This involves grazing your animals in sequence on a specific parcel of land that is just one pasture of many on your site. You work that parcel for a time and then move on to another when you are ready (likely just a few days or so). For example, the cows would be let in first. While eating their fill of grass, they would stomp on and grind down dead plants and deposit manure. Chickens would follow afterward, helping distribute the cow manure across the parcel and feeding on parasitic larvae that might endanger the cows later. Other animals might also be worked into the chain.

Permaculture-Friendly Animals

Cats: Cats are one of the most common domesticated animals. They help keep mice and rats under control, as well as a few other small animals. Beyond that, they make excellent companions.

Chickens: Chickens are an excellent choice because they are extremely versatile. They not only serve well on rural farms, but (if the laws permit) they can even be incorporated on sites in more urban areas. As for benefits, they feed on bugs, fruit maggots, and other pests. They are a source of meat, eggs, feathers, and manure. They also scratch up land to break up the soil.

Cows: Cows have a lot of yields. First, they eat a lot of grass, so they serve as nature's lawnmowers. This grass, in turn, becomes manure that can be used to fertilize your plants and trees. Additionally, cows produce milk which can also be turned into cheese, butter, cream, and yogurt. Finally, they can also be used as food.

Dogs: Dogs have several uses. They can help control and protect other animals through herding. They can sound the alarm when an intruder approaches. And, like cats, they are excellent companion animals. However, some dogs may kill chickens and other small animals, so you have to be a little careful with them.

Donkeys: Donkeys are great because they can do farm work and, much like horses, eat a lot of grass and weeds, transforming foliage into rich, useful manure to feed your compost piles and soil. They also make wonderful companions.

Ducks: Ducks are a little more restrained than chickens are when it comes to your vegetable patch, so that's an added bonus. They also eat a number of pesky critters like snails and other small insects that chickens don't eat. So between the two of them, ducks and chickens, they offer excellent all-around pest protection—what one doesn't eat, the other likely will. Finally, they offer meat and feathers as resources, too.

Fish: Fish feed on plants, worms, and other little critters you might find in the water. Afterward, when they produce excrement, it spreads throughout the water. So, when you use this water for your gardens and other lands, it provides a higher load of nutrients to both the soil and the vegetables or fruits you are growing. And, of course, fish can also be used as food for yourself or for some of your other animals.

Geese: Geese feed on grass which they turn into droppings that, unlike many other types of manure, don't smell bad. They are a great form of poultry to raise inside a food forest as there are many vegetables they do not eat. Similarly, they don't generally turn grassy pastures into muddy areas as other animals can. Finally, they also serve to warn about intruders, making them great guard animals.

Goats: Goats are another excellent choice for a permaculture animal. They eat weeds, shrubs, and other greenery, eating even the prickliest plants that can be hard to handle by hand. You do need to be careful with them, though, as they can threaten healthy trees and eat them if there is no other source of food. But they are well-known for producing excellent milk, which can be made into delicious cheese. You have to be careful with goats, though, because they do have a tendency to escape when given a chance.

Pigs: Pigs feed on a wide variety of foods, including acorns, weeds, scraps, and most anything remotely edible. Their manure is also useful for soil and compost. They can also be used to dig up some types of deep-rooted weeds that otherwise might be a nuisance to deal with. You simply bury an acorn or other treat in the spot you want the pig to dig and let them have at it. This saves on the wear and tear and environmental discharge from whatever machine you might have otherwise used for the job.

Rabbits: When rabbits are placed in a cage that lacks a bottom, the cage and rabbits can be moved from spot to spot to keep the grass from growing too high. Likewise, their manure serves to fertilize the grass or whatever plants might be growing there.

Sheep: If you are wary of the potential damage goats might cause, then selecting sheep for your site might be the way to go. They do far less damage, and they produce a number of yields: lambs, wool, milk, cheese, and manure, to name just a few.

Snails: Some snails can be problematic and might become pests for your garden. Others are edible. If you don't want to eat them, there is a good chance your ducks will.

Worms: Like chickens, worms can be used in urban areas. Worms can be raised in the smallest of spaces, provided there is some type of climate control. With vermicomposting, worms can turn leftover kitchen scraps like vegetables and fruits into rich soil and Worm Tea (a kind of liquid fertilizer). In addition to indoor composting, worms can be used in your gardens too. They tunnel through and aerate your soil, while providing an excellent snack for poultry.

Although raising animals requires more resources per calorie than raising plants, it is also true that it can be difficult to meet all your nutritional requirements with only plants. You also need to factor in the yields animals give that plants cannot match. They can be used for food, clothing, pest control, yard work, and more. Every ecosystem found in nature incorporates animals at some level, so it's a good idea to plan on using animals in some fashion on your permaculture site. Even if you don't wind up eating them, they will still serve many useful interrelated roles on your land.

Conclusion

So, now that you've reached the end of the book, hopefully you've gotten a clearer picture on what permaculture is and how you can incorporate it into your life for the best results. What you ultimately need to remember is that the idea behind permaculture is to find a sort of balance between yourself and the world around you. It's a way to look at the world in a more "shareable" context than just "take, take, take." With everything covered in the book, this should be more doable for everyone.

What you hopefully come out of this with is a better understanding of how you can work with the world around you, and not just have it work for you. To reiterate, let's remember that three tenets of permaculture. Care for the earth, and we cannot say that enough. Care for the people around you, because the world works best when there's a balance and we don't act like we're isolated islands. And of course, take your fair share and return the excess. Always remember that there's a huge difference between what we want and what we need.

We've talked about the Twelve Principles of permaculture, and how important they are to the world around us. Sure, elements like "produce no waste" might seem difficult at first, but with the right mindset, anything can be done. You need to remember that it's all about working together with the world around you to maintain the most favorable balance.

We've also gone over the benefits of permaculture. How there is no comparison to eating healthier food. How costs are drastically reduced for you and your family. How less waste and less pollution is produced, and in turn, we are a benefit to Mother Nature instead of a burden. How through permaculture we can encourage diversity and improve the environment.

We've discussed how to design the right permaculture space, taking sector analysis and zoning into account. We've talked about designing your mainframe, providing the right access, and making use of your space. Of course, you need to always remember that it's important to maintain a relationship between the different components of your permaculture world.

You've also been introduced to the major importance of solar power and how this renewable energy source can make all the difference. Plus, composting and how we can reuse the waste we produce in ways that give back to the environment.

The goal of permaculture is to be sustainable. Animals are a part of that goal, as are plants, sunlight, water management, and the many other topics discussed in this book. Together, they offer a path to permaculture freedom. A path to help the world work towards solving the climate crisis while providing a roadmap for individuals to create a self-sufficient environment at home. Anyone can benefit from permaculture practices, whether you live on a rural farm or in a sprawling urban center. This book is offered as a map and a guidebook, with the hope and intent of making the world an eco-friendlier place and your backyard a plethora of riches.

As you set out on your own permaculture journey, may you have the best of luck.

Here's another book by Dion Rosser that you might like

References

7 uses of solar energy. (2018, July 12). Retrieved from Freedomsolarpower.com website: https://freedomsolarpower.com/blog/7-uses-of-solar-energy

12 principles of Permaculture by David Holmgren. (2010, January 14). Retrieved from Wordpress.com website: https://justlists.wordpress.com/2010/01/14/principles-of-permaculture/

Agritecture. (2019, May 28). 10 Benefits Of Urban Permaculture. Retrieved from Agritecture.com website: https://www.agritecture.com/blog/2019/5/28/10-benefits-of-urban-permaculture

All About Composting: Learn how to compost from Gardener's Supply. (n.d.). Retrieved from Gardeners.com website: https://www.gardeners.com/how-to/all-about-composting/5061.html

Animals in ecosystems. (2015, March 22). Retrieved from Permacultureartisans.com website: http://www.permacultureartisans.com/permaculture-building/animals-ecosystems/

Ashley. (2017, October 2). Your guide to urban composting. Retrieved from Purplecarrot.com website: https://www.purplecarrot.com/blog/composting-in-the-city/

Baker, L. (2020, October 28). 10 home items you can reuse over and over again - one green planet. Retrieved from Onegreenplanet.org website: https://www.onegreenplanet.org/lifestyle/home-items-you-can-reuse-over-and-over-again/

Chapter 7: Water. (2010, December 21). Retrieved from Treeyopermacultureedu.com website: https://treeyopermacultureedu.com/chapter-7-water/

Difference between organic gardening and Permaculture. (2013, July 1). Retrieved from Permaculturevisions.com website: https://permaculturevisions.com/the-difference-between-organic-gardening-and-permaculture/

Editors, B. G. (2016, May 26). Your step-by-step guide to making compost that will enrich your garden. Retrieved from Bhg.com website: https://www.bhg.com/gardening/yard/compost/how-to-compost/

Footsteps, C. @. T. (2014, January 10). Permaculture for urban homes and small spaces. Retrieved from Theselightfootsteps.com website: https://theselightfootsteps.com/2014/01/10/permaculture-for-urban-homes-and-small-spaces/

Garden Design Magazine. (2020, March 11). Annual vs perennial – what is the difference? - garden design. Retrieved from Gardendesign.com website: https://www.gardendesign.com/annuals/vs-perennials.html

Hendry, A. M. (n.d.). Permaculture for Small Gardens. Retrieved from Growveg.com website: https://www.growveg.com/guides/permaculture-for-small-gardens/

Horvat, H. (2017, April 17). Water management for every permaculture farm - permaculture apprentice. Retrieved from Permacultureapprentice.com website: https://permacultureapprentice.com/permaculture-water-management/

How to start your Permaculture garden. (2010, November 26). Retrieved from Deepgreenpermaculture.com website:

https://deepgreenpermaculture.com/diy-instructions/starting-your-permaculture-garden/

Integrating animals on a permaculture farm. (n.d.). Retrieved from Keelayogafarm.com website: https://www.keelayogafarm.com/permaculture/integrating-animals-on-a-permaculture-farm/

Jillian Levy, C. (2017, September 29). Diagram shows how to create your very own "food forest" (better than organic!). Retrieved from Draxe.com website:

https://draxe.com/health/permaculture/

Jim, U. (2016, February 22). What are the different kinds of composting? - uncle Jim's worm farm. Retrieved from Unclejimswormfarm.com website:

https://unclejimswormfarm.com/different-kinds-composting/

joie. (2020, April 2). How greenhouses work: Tips and tricks. Retrieved from Properlyrooted.com website: https://properlyrooted.com/how-does-greenhouse-work/

Kathryn. (2016, April 29). 11 reasons why you need to know about permaculture. Retrieved from Farmingmybackyard.com website: https://farmingmybackyard.com/permaculture/

Lanier, K. (2014, December 12). 6 unique features of permaculture greenhouses - hobby farms. Retrieved from Hobbyfarms.com website: https://www.hobbyfarms.com/6-unique-features-of-permaculture-greenhouses-3/

Lyons, S. (n.d.). What is a permaculture garden and how do I start one? Retrieved from Thespruce.com website: https://www.thespruce.com/how-to-start-a-permaculture-garden-4050110

Meyer, E. (2017, October 18). The 12 design principles of permaculture as rules of living. Retrieved from Land And Ladle website: https://medium.com/land-and-ladle/the-12-design-principles-of-permaculture-as-rules-of-living-e9fc0176dd16

Noel. (2014, August 25). 7 ideas for urban permaculture. Retrieved from Regenerative.com website: https://regenerative.com/seven-ideas-urban-permaculture/

Permaculture design principle 6: Design scale and use of space. (n.d.). Retrieved from Tropicalpermaculture.com website: https://www.tropicalpermaculture.com/permaculture-design-principles-6.html

Permaculture magazine. (2013, January 30). Retrieved from Permaculture.co.uk website: https://www.permaculture.co.uk/articles/what-permaculture-part-2-principles

Permaculture: You've heard of it, but what the heck is it? (2016, April 19). Retrieved from Modernfarmer.com website: https://modernfarmer.com/2016/04/permaculture/

Rainwater harvesting: 8 methods. (2018, July 20). Retrieved from Worldpermacultureassociation.com website: https://worldpermacultureassociation.com/rainwater-harvesting-8-methods/

Recycling and Permaculture. (n.d.). Retrieved from Sandia.org website: https://www.sandia.org/recycling-and-permaculture

Sayner, A. (2020, January 21). How to start A permaculture garden: Beginner's guide - GroCycle. Retrieved from Grocycle.com website: https://grocycle.com/how-to-start-a-permaculture-garden/

Shallert, L. (2013, October 15). Year-round greenhouse - Midwest permaculture. Retrieved from Midwestpermaculture.com website: https://midwestpermaculture.com/2013/10/year-round-greenhouse-2/

Solar panels 101: Your guide to solar energy basics. (2019, October 16). Retrieved from Unboundsolar.com website: https://unboundsolar.com/solar-information/solar-power-101

Solar Power Authority Staff. (2010, July 15). 5 easy ways to get started with solar power. Retrieved from Solarpowerauthority.com website: https://www.solarpowerauthority.com/easy-and-affordable-ways-to-start-using-solar-today/

Tenth Acre Farm. (2015, April 21). What is permaculture? Design a garden that works with nature. Retrieved from Tenthacrefarm.com website: https://www.tenthacrefarm.com/what-is-permaculture/

Tilley, N. (2007, May 30). Permaculture gardens - benefits of permaculture gardening. Retrieved from Gardeningknowhow.com website: https://www.gardeningknowhow.com/special/organic/the-essence-of-permaculture-gardening.htm

USI Web Services. (n.d.). Solid waste & landfill facts - university of southern Indiana. Retrieved from Usi.edu website: https://www.usi.edu/recycle/solid-waste-landfill-facts/

Waddington, E. (2019, April 23). The 12 principles of permaculture: A way forward. Retrieved from Ethical.net website: https://ethical.net/ethical/permaculture-principles/

Water management. (2015, March 22). Retrieved from Permacultureartisans.com website: http://www.permacultureartisans.com/permaculture-building/water-management/

What are the Benefits of Permaculture? You'll Be Amazed to Know (2011, September 29). Retrieved from Gardenerdy.com website: https://gardenerdy.com/what-are-benefits-of-permaculture/

(N.d.-a). Retrieved from Permaculturenews.org website: https://www.permaculturenews.org/what-is-permaculture/

(N.d.-b). Retrieved from Permaculturenews.org website:

https://www.permaculturenews.org/2016/03/07/permaculture-animals-as-a-discipline-to-the-system/

(N.d.-c). Retrieved from Permaculturenews.org website:

https://www.permaculturenews.org/2016/03/11/5-simple-ideas-for-transitioning-into-a-permaculture-garden/

(N.d.-d). Retrieved from Permaculturenews.org website:

https://www.permaculturenews.org/2017/09/05/permaculture-design-5-steps/

(N.d.-e). Retrieved from Hgtv.com website:

https://www.hgtv.com/design/remodel/mechanical-systems/getting-started-with-diy-solar-power

(N.d.-f). Retrieved from Permaculturenews.org website:

https://www.permaculturenews.org/2014/05/13/constructively-reducing-waste/

Printed in Great Britain
by Amazon

70535349R00078